U.S. Naval Vessels
A Military Photo Logbook

Volume 1

D0851681

COMPILED BY
DENNIS R. JENKINS

specialtypress
PUBLISHERS AND WHOLESALERS

ISBN 978-1-58007-115-4

Item Number SP115

SPECIALTY PRESS
PUBLISHERS AND WHOLESALERS

39966 Grand Avenue
North Branch, MN 55056 USA
(651) 277-1400 or (800) 895-4585
www.specialtypress.com

Printed in China

Distributed in the UK and Europe by:

Midland Publishing
4 Watling Drive
Hinckley LE10 3EY, England
Tel: 01455 233 747 Fax: 01455 233 737
www.midlandcountiessuperstore.com

On the Cover, Left: *07 October 2006, Pacific Ocean – A Parade of Ships led by the nuclear-powered aircraft carrier USS Nimitz (CVN 68) prepares to pass under the Golden Gate Bridge while entering the bay for San Francisco Fleet Week 2006.* (U.S. Navy photo by Mass Communication Specialist 3rd Class Roland Franklin)

On the Cover, Top Right: *13 January 2006, Pacific Ocean – The guided missile destroyer USS Decatur (DDG 73) comes along side the oiler (TAO 197) during a replenishment at sea.* (U.S. Navy photo by Photographer's Mate Airman Kathleen Gorby)

On the Cover, Bottom Right: *03 October 2006, Norfolk, Virginia – Nuclear, fast-attack submarines USS Minneapolis-St. Paul (SSN 708) and USS Newport News (SSN 750) prepare to get underway for a scheduled six-month deployment as part of the Eisenhower Carrier Strike Group.* (U.S. Navy photo by Mass Communication Specialists 1st Class Christina M. Shaw)

On the Back Cover, Upper Left: *07 July 2006, Pacific Ocean – A Standard Missile 2 (SM-2) launches from the aft Vertical Launching System (VLS) aboard the guided-missile destroyer USS O'Kane (DDG 77). The launch was part of a live-fire exercise while participating in the Rim of the Pacific (RIMPAC) 2006 biennial maritime exercise.* (U.S. Navy photo by Mass Communications Specialist Third Class Marcos T. Hernandez)

On the Back Cover, Lower Left: *17 May 2006, Gulf of Mexico – The ex-Oriskany, a decommissioned aircraft carrier, was sunk 24 miles off the coast of Pensacola, Florida, to form an artificial reef. The 888-foot ship took about 37 minutes to sink below the surface. After 25 years of service to the Navy in operations in Korea, Vietnam, and the Mediterranean, ex-Oriskany will now benefit marine life and recreation diving off the Florida panhandle.* (U.S. Navy photo by Photographer's Mate 2nd Class Jeffrey P. Kraus)

On the Back Cover, Lower Right: *10 February 2006, Pearl Harbor, Hawaii – The amphibious transport dock ship USS Cleveland (LPD 7) prepares to moor at Pearl Harbor for a brief port visit on its return from a seven-month deployment.* (U.S. Navy photo by Journalist 2nd Class Ryan C. McGinley)

On the Title Page: *05 May 2006, Persian Gulf – The guided missile destroyer USS McCampbell (DDG 85) comes alongside the aircraft carrier USS Ronald Reagan (CVN 76) for a routine fueling at sea.* (U.S. Navy photo by Photographer's Mate 1st Class James Thierry)

CONTENTS

INTRODUCTION

The United States Navy traces its origins to the Continental Navy, which was established during the American Revolutionary War and disbanded in 1790. Nevertheless, the United States Constitution allowed Congress "to provide and maintain a navy" which it did by passing the Naval Act of 1794 and ordering the construction and manning of six frigates.

The U.S. Navy came into international prominence in the 20th Century, especially during World War II. Operating in both the European and Pacific theatres, it was a part of the conflict from the onset of American military involvement — the attack on Pearl Harbor — to Japan's official surrender on the deck of the USS *Missouri* in Tokyo Bay. The Navy had a pivotal role in the subsequent Cold War, in which it evolved into a nuclear deterrent and crisis response force while preparing for a possible global war with the Soviet Union.

The United States Navy maintains a sizeable presence throughout the world, deploying in such areas as East Asia, Southern Europe, and the Middle East. Its ability to project force onto the littoral regions of the world, engage in forward areas during peacetime, and rapidly respond to regional crises makes it an active player in American policy. Despite decreases in ships and personnel following the Cold War, the Navy has continued to spend more on technology than any other and is the world's largest navy with a tonnage greater than that of the next dozen largest navies combined.

The U.S. Coast Guard is one of the oldest organizations of the federal government and, until the Navy Department was established, it served as the nation's only armed force afloat. In times of peace the Coast Guard operates as part of the Department of Homeland Security. In times of war, or on direction of the President, it serves under the Navy Department.

Like all organizations, the Navy and Coast Guard take pride recording their accomplishments and employs a large team of professional photographers as well as many amateurs. These photographers have few restrictions placed on them about what or when they shoot (although many photographs are never released due to security concerns). The images they capture tend to concentrate on people and events because that is the essence of any organization. Nevertheless, the hardware gets its fair share of exposure, and that is the emphasis of this book.

Military photographers or service members took the photographs contained herein and show the Navy as it exists, in its glory and its sadness, in peace and at war. The captions are edited versions of what the photographer wrote – sometimes I would have emphasized a different aspect of the photograph, but it was not my choice. Often the photographs exist in a vacuum, with little context – there might be a detail shot of a a weapon with no corresponding overall photo of the ship. This is how the Navy released the photo. Other times, the photos trace a story, for instance the purposeful sinking of the former USS *Oriskany* and the construction of the Coast Guard cutter *Bertholf*.

The 300-plus photographs represent a cross-section of the Navy and what it accomplished during 2006. The photographs are presented in roughly chronological order (a few liberties were taken to allow a clean layout for the book) and attempt to show a balanced view, but that is for the reader to ultimately decide.

Dennis R. Jenkins
Cape Canaveral, Florida

04 January 2006, Coronado, California – Sailors aboard the USS Ronald Reagan (CVN 76) man the rails as it departs Naval Air Station North Island. This was the maiden operational deployment for the Navy's newest Nimitz-Class nuclear powered aircraft carrier and her 5,500-man crew. (U.S. Navy photo by Photographer's Mate 2nd Class Christopher Brown)

04 January 2006, Coronado, California – Two Sikorsky SH-60F Seahawks assigned to HS-4 Black Knights provide security for the USS Ronald Reagan (CVN 76) while departing North Island. (U.S. Navy photo by Photographer's Mate 2nd Class Christopher Brown)

04 January 2006, Coronado, California – The water washdown system is tested on the USS Ronald Reagan (CVN 76) as it leaves San Diego on its first cruise. (U.S. Navy photo by Photographer's Mate 2nd Class Christopher Brown)

09 January 2006, Pearl Harbor, Hawaii – Sailors aboard USS Chosin (CG 65) man the rails as they return home after a deployment to the Persian Gulf. (U.S. Navy photo by Photographer's Mate 3rd Class TeResa R. Martinez)

05 January 2006, Point Pleasant, New Jersey – A U.S. Coast Guard rescue crew from Station Manasquan Inlet underway during training. (U.S. Coast Guard photo by PAC Tom Sperduto)

10 January 2006, Naval Base Point Loma, California – *The crew of the only commissioned floating dry-dock, Arco (ARDM-5), pulls the USS Helena (SSN 725) into the dry-dock for routine scheduled maintenance.* (U.S. Navy photo by Journalist Seaman Joseph Caballero)

09 January 2006, Pearl Harbor, Hawaii – The heavy lift vessel MV Blue Marlin enters Pearl Harbor, Hawaii, with the Sea Based X-Band Radar (SBX) aboard after completing a 15,000-mile journey from Corpus Christi, Texas. SBX is a combination of the world's largest phased array X-band radar carried aboard a mobile, ocean-going semi-submersible oil platform. It will provide accurate and early ballistic missile detection and will be able to discriminate a hostile warhead from decoys and countermeasures. SBX will undergo minor modifications, post-transit maintenance and routine inspections in Pearl Harbor before completing its voyage to its home port of Adak, Alaska in the Aleutian Islands. (U.S. Navy photo by Chief Journalist Joe Kane)

11 January 2006, Pacific Ocean – A Grumman E-2C Hawkeye from the "Black Eagles" of VAW-113 launches from the USS Ronald Reagan (CVN 76) during an anti-submarine warfare exercise off the coast of Hawaii. Reagan was on her maiden deployment in support of maritime security operations. (U.S. Navy photo by Photographer's Mate Airman Kathleen Gorby)

12 January 2006, Washington, D.C. – An artist concept of the Fast Response Cutter (FRC) being procured as part of the Deepwater program. It will be able to deploy independently to conduct a large range of multiple missions including fishery patrols, law enforcement, maritime security, search and rescue, and defense operations. (U.S. Coast Guard illustration courtesy of Northrop Grumman)

12 January 2006, Souda Bay, Crete, Greece – The U.S. Navy High-Speed Vessel (HSV-2) Swift departs the Marathi NATO pier facility following a brief port visit. Swift is assigned to the Mine Warfare Command in Ingleside, Texas, and is operated by two rotating 42-person crews. A Gold-crew, based at Little Creek, Virginia, concentrates on expeditionary missions while a Blue-crew from Ingleside, focuses on mine warfare. At 321 feet, Swift has a top speed of almost 50 knots. The catamaran's aluminum hulls draw only about 11 feet of water, making the ship ideal for missions in shallow coastal regions. (U.S. Navy photo by Mr. Paul Farley)

13 January 2006, Pacific Ocean – The guided-missile destroyer USS Decatur (DDG 73) comes along side the Military Sealift Command (MSC) oiler USNA Pecos (TAO 197) during a replenishment at sea. (U.S. Navy photo by Photographer's Mate Airman Kathleen Gorby)

14 January 2006, Pacific Ocean – Two MH-60S Seahawk helicopters assigned to the "Blackjacks" of HSC-21 carry supplies from the fast combat support ship USNS Bridge (T-AOE 10) to the flight deck aboard the Nimitz-class aircraft carrier USS Abraham Lincoln (CVN 72) during an underway replenishment. Lincoln is currently off the coast of Southern California for flight operation training. (U.S. Navy photos by Photographer's Mate Airman Justin R. Blake and Mary E. Guiney)

15 January 2006, Monrovia, Liberia – The Oliver Hazard Perry-class frigate USS Carr (FFG 52) visited Monrovia to commemorate the inauguration of President Ellen Johnson Sirleaf. The 30-knot class uses a pair of General Electric LM2500-30 gas turbines generating 41,000 shp driving a single variable pitch propeller. Carr is home-ported out of Norfolk, Virginia. (U.S. Navy photo by Journalist 1st Class Kurt Riggs)

14 January 2006, Eastern Atlantic – The command and control ship USS Mount Whitney (LCC 20) is the flagship for Commander Naval Forces Europe-Commander Sixth Fleet (CNE-C6F). (U.S. Navy Photo by Journalist 1st Class Kurt Riggs)

18 January 2006, Sagami-Wan, Japan – The amphibious command ship USS Blue Ridge (LCC 19) transits the eastern coast of Japan as Mt. Fuji looms on the horizon. (U.S. Navy photo by Aviation Warfare Systems Operator 2nd Class Roger Moore)

17 January 2006, Atlantic Coast – A SEAL delivery vehicle (SDV) team works topside after conducting training drills with Sailors assigned to the Los Angeles-class fast-attack submarine USS Toledo (SSN 769). SDV teams' missions include clandestine insertion of SEALs, ordnance delivery, location and recovery of objects, and reconnaissance. (U.S. Navy photo by Journalist 3rd Class Davis J. Anderson)

17 January 2006, Atlantic Coast – A SEAL delivery vehicle team (SDV) perform a fast-roping exercise from a MH-60S Seahawk helicopter to the topside of the Toledo (SSN 769). (U.S. Navy photo by Journalist 3rd Class Davis J. Anderson)

17 January 2006, Manama, Bahrain – The Los Angeles-class fast attack submarine USS Norfolk (SSN 714) is moored to the Mina Salman Pier in Bahrain during a brief port visit. (U.S. Navy photo by Photographer's Mate 2nd Class Carolla Bennett)

31 January 2006, San Diego, California – The Seahorse-class Autonomous Underwater Vehicle (AUV) is maneuvered into position in Sea Fighter's (FSF-1) mission bay during launch and recovery testing. At 28 feet, 6 inches, and weighing 10,800 pounds, Seahorse is an untethered, unmanned, underwater robotic vehicle, capable of pre-programmed independent operations. The Office of Naval Research (ONR) sponsored the demonstrations. (U.S. Navy photo by Mr. John F. Williams)

30 January 2006, Sydney, Australia – The guided missile destroyer USS Pinckney (DDG 91) transits past the Sydney Opera house while participating in the Pacific 2006 International Maritime Exposition. (Royal Australian Navy photo by Able Seaman Paul Berry)

30 January 2006, Pearl Harbor, Hawaii – The Japanese Defense Ship (JDS) Oyashio, lead submarine of the Oyashio class, conducted exercises and training with the U.S. Navy in the Pearl Harbor region. (U.S. Navy photo by Journalist 2nd Class Ryan C. McGinley)

06 February 2006, Atlantic Ocean – Ammunition is transferred from the flight deck to the ship's hangar bay during loading operations aboard the USS George Washington (CVN 73). (U.S. Navy photo by Photographer's Mate Airman Rex Nelson)

11 February 2006, Pacific Ocean – The USS Nimitz (CVN 68) transits the Pacific Ocean in preparation for a major propulsion plant evaluation off the coast of southern California. (U.S. Navy photo by Photographer's Mate 3rd Class Shannon E. Renfroe)

06 February 2006, Norfolk, Virginia – A SEAL Delivery Vehicle (SDV) is loaded aboard the Los Angeles-class fast attack submarine USS Dallas (SSN 700) in preparation for a Special Warfare Training exercise. SDV is a "wet" submersible, designed to carry SEALs and their cargo in fully flooded compartments. A Dry Deck Shelter (DDS) is attached to the submarine's rear escape trunk to carry the SDV. (U.S. Navy photo by Chief Journalist Dave Fliesen)

06 February 2006, Atlantic Ocean – The aircraft carrier USS Enterprise (CVN 65) conducts a refueling at sea with the guided missile destroyer USS McFaul (DDG 74). Although the nuclear-powered Enterprise does not require fuel, it carries a considerable amount for its aircraft and escort ships. Enterprise was conducting routine carrier qualifications. (U.S. Navy photo by Photographer's Mate 3rd Class Josh Kinter)

10 February 2006, Pearl Harbor, Hawaii – Crew members aboard the Los Angeles-class fast attack submarine USS Louisville (SSN 724) man the submarine's sail as they return to their home port after completing routine training. (U.S. Navy photo by Journalist 2nd Class Ryan C. McGinley)

10 February 2006, Pearl Harbor, Hawaii – The amphibious transport dock ship USS Cleveland (LPD 7) prepares to moor for a brief port visit on its return from a seven-month deployment in support Operation Iraqi Freedom. (U.S. Navy photo by Journalist 2nd Class Ryan C. McGinley)

13 February 2006, Rota, Spain – An Army CH-47 Chinook helicopter is unloaded from the USNS Pililaau. The helicopter will be loaded onto a U.S. Air Force C-17 Globemaster III for transportation to Southwest Asia. (U. S. Air Force Photo by Senior Airman Nichole Adamowicz)

15 February 2006, Antarctica – The Coast Guard Cutter Polar Star breaks ice in the turning basin outside McMurdo Station. (U.S. Coast Guard photo by PA2 Mariana O'Leary)

15 February 2006, Suez Canal – The Nimitz-class aircraft carrier USS Theodore Roosevelt (CVN 71) transits through the 100-mile Suez Canal that connects the Red Sea and the Mediterranean Sea. Roosevelt and Carrier Air Wing Eight (CVW-8) were underway on a regularly scheduled deployment supporting maritime security operations. (U.S. Navy photo by Photographer's Mate Airman Javier Capella)

15 February 2006, Philippine Sea – The amphibious assault ship USS Essex (LHD 2) and the amphibious transport dock ship USS Juneau (LPD 10) refuel with the underway replenishment oiler USNS Walter S. Diehl (T-AO 193). (U.S. Navy photo by Journalist 2nd Class Brian P. Biller)

16 February 2006, Persian Gulf – The amphibious dock landing ship USS Carter Hall (LSD 50) approaches the oiler USNS Rappahannock (T-AO 204) and the amphibious assault ship USS Nassau (LHA 4) for a connected replenishment during maritime security operations. (U.S. Navy photo by Photographer's Mate 2nd Class Michael J. Sandberg)

16 February 2006, Antarctica – The Coast Guard Cutter Polar Star sits hove-to on the ice outside McMurdo Station, while the crew enjoys ice liberty. (U.S. Coast Guard photo by PA2 Mariana O'Leary)

16 February 2006, Souda Bay, Crete, Greece – The Los Angeles-class submarine USS Annapolis (SSN 760) prepares to depart the pier following a routine port visit. (U.S. Navy photo by Mr. Paul Farley)

01 March 2006, Yokosuka, Japan – Yokosuka Port Operations pusher boats and a U. S. Navy tugboat move the guided missile destroyer USS Fitzgerald (DDG 62) pier-side after she recently completed a scheduled maintenance period. (U.S. Navy photo by Photographer's Mate Airman Patrick L. Heil)

03 March 2006, Atlantic Ocean – An HH-60 Seahawk transfers supplies from the fast combat support ship USNS Supply (T-AOE-6) to the nuclear-powered aircraft carrier USS Enterprise (CVN 65) during a replenishment at sea. (U.S. Navy photo by Photographer's Mate Airman Marshall James)

01 March 2006, Portsmouth, Virginia – The 270-foot medium endurance Cutter Harriet Lane ties up after returning from a homeland security patrol. (U.S. Coast Guard photo by PA3 Kip Wadlow)

01 March 2006, Cabalian Bay, Republic of the Philippines – This Landing Craft Air Cushioned (LCAC) was assigned to Assault Craft Unit Five (ACU-5) aboard USS Essex (LHD 2). (U.S. Navy photo by Photographer's Mate 1st Class Michael D. Kennedy)

08 March 2006, Pacific Ocean – An SM-3 missile is launched from the Ticonderoga-class cruiser USS Lake Erie (CG 70) during a Missile Defense Agency test of the Japanese-designed advanced nosecone and Aegis ballistic missile defense system. (U.S. Navy photo)

09 March 2006, Newport News, Virginia – The Virginia-class nuclear fast attack submarine North Carolina (SSN 777) under construction at Northrop Grumman Newport News shipyard. North Carolina is the fourth Virginia-class submarine and is scheduled to join the fleet in 2008. The class is supplanting the long-serving Los Angeles class. (Photo by Mr. John Whalen courtesy Northrop Grumman Ship Building)

14 May 2006, Pacific Ocean – The Nimitz-class nuclear-powered aircraft carrier USS John C. Stennis (CVN 74) conducting air group qualifications off the coast of Southern California. A variety of Northrop Grumman EA-6B Prowlers and Boeing F/A-18 Hornets, including a camouflaged one, are parked on the flight deck. (U.S. Navy photo by Photographer's Mate Airman Paul J. Perkins)

15 March 2006, Newport News, Virginia – At upper left, on 9 March 2006 the island upper levels were placed upon the lower levels to complete the island structure. The other photographs show the upper bow unit of the Pre-Commissioning Unit (PCU) George H.W. Bush (CVN 77) being lifted into place. The nuclear-powered aircraft carrier is under construction at Northrop Grumman Newport News shipyard. CVN 77 is the tenth and last Nimitz-class aircraft carrier and is scheduled to be delivered to the U.S. Navy in 2008. (Photos by Mr. John Whalen courtesy Northrop Grumman Ship Building)

15 March 2006, Seal Beach, California – Naval Weapons Station Seal Beach Standard Missile Shop technician Joshua Jackson performs maintenance on an SM-2 Standard surface-to-air missile. (U.S. Navy photo by Eleno Cortez)

17 March 2006, South China Sea – The amphibious command ship USS Blue Ridge (LCC 19) is the 7th Fleet command ship, underway on a regularly scheduled deployment. (U.S. Navy photo by Journalist Seaman Marc Rockwell-Pate)

22 March 2006, Pensacola, Florida – Tugboats turn the decommissioned aircraft carrier USS Oriskany (CVA 34) prior to mooring at Allegheny Pier at Naval Air Station Pensacola. Known as the "Big O," the 32,000-ton, 888-foot Oriskany is being delivered to Pensacola, where it is being prepared for its final journey. Oriskany is scheduled to be scuttled 24 miles south of Pensacola in approximately 212 feet of water in the Gulf of Mexico on 17 May 2006, where it will become the largest ship ever intentionally sunk as an artificial reef. After the Oriskany reaches the bottom, ownership of the vessel will transfer from the Navy to the State of Florida. (U.S. Navy photo by Megan Kohr)

22 March 2006, Sea of Japan – An Amphibious Assault Vehicle (AAV) assigned to the 31st Marine Expeditionary Unit (MEU) approaches the well deck of the amphibious dock landing ship USS Harpers Ferry (LSD 49). (U.S. Navy photo by Journalist 2nd Class Brian P. Biller)

27 March 2006, Pacific Ocean – The underway replenishment oiler USNS Walter S. Diehl (T-AO 193) and the ammunition ship USNS Shasta (T-AE 33) pull away from the USS Abraham Lincoln (CVN 72). (U.S. Navy photo by Photographer's Mate 3rd Class James R. McGury)

30 March 2006, Yokosuka, Japan – A harbor tug assists the nuclear-powered attack submarine USS Tucson (SSN 770) as it arrives at Commander, Fleet Activities Yokosuka, Japan. Tucson departed on a six-month Western Pacific deployment from its home port of Pearl Harbor. (U.S. Navy photo by Photographer's Mate 2nd Class Chantel M. Clayton)

31 March 2006, Atlantic Ocean – The guided-missile submarine USS Florida (SSGN 728) conducts sea trials off the coast of Virginia. Florida is scheduled to return to service in May 2006 as the second of four submarines to be converted from a ballistic missile submarine (SSBN) to the new class of guided missile submarines (SSGN). (U.S. Navy photo by Chief Journalist Dave Fliesen)

31 March 2006, Norfolk, Virginia – The guided-missile submarine USS Florida (SSGN 728) will have the capability to launch up to 154 Tomahawk cruise missiles, conduct sustained special forces operations and carry other payloads, such as unmanned underwater vehicles (UUV), unmanned aerial vehicles (UAV) and special forces equipment. (U.S. Navy photo by Chief Journalist Dave Fliesen)

31 March 2006, Yellow Sea – The Ticonderoga-class guided-missile cruiser USS Chosin (CG 65) and the Russian Navy Udaloy-class destroyer Marshal Shaposhnikov (DDGHM 543) sail in formation during a joint Russian-U.S. Navy exercise. The Russian Federation Navy made the first visit of a Russian Navy vessel to the U.S. territory of Guam to participate in a joint humanitarian assistance and disaster relief exercise. (U.S. Navy photo by Photographer's Mate 2nd Class Nathanael T. Miller)

04 April 2006, Atlantic Ocean – The conventionally-powered aircraft carrier USS John F. Kennedy (CV 67) conducts live fire training using the 20-millimeter Phalanx Close-In Weapons System (CIWS). (U.S. Navy photo by Photographer's Mate 3rd Class Erica Treider)

12 April 2006, East China Sea – The amphibious dock landing ship USS Harpers Ferry (LSD 49) launches chaff from a Mk 36 Super Rapid Blooming Outboard Chaff launcher during combat systems readiness drills. (U.S. Navy photo by Fire Controlman 1st Class)

06 April 2006, Everett, Washington – Sailors stationed aboard the guided missile destroyer USS Momsen (DDG 92) man the rails as the ship pulls away from her home port of Naval Station Everett. Momsen and her crew were underway for their maiden deployment. The ship is the 14th Flight IIA Arleigh Burke-class ship and was commissioned on 28 August 2004. (U.S. Navy photo by Photographer's Mate 3rd Class Douglas G. Morrison)

14 April 2006, Persian Gulf – The Cyclone-class coastal patrol craft USS Whirlwind (PC 11) monitors Iraq's oil terminals in the Northern Persian Gulf as part of Operation Iraqi Freedom. (U.S. Navy photo by Journalist 2nd Class Zack Baddorf)

16 April 2006, South China Sea – The guided missile cruiser USS Mobile Bay (CG 53) and destroyer USS Russell (DDG 59) protect the flank of the aircraft carrier USS Abraham Lincoln (CVN 72). (U.S. Navy photo by Photographer's Mate Airman Timothy C. Roache Jr.)

20 April 2006, Caribbean Sea – The guided-missile cruiser USS Monterey (CG 61) prepares to conduct a fueling at sea with the air-craft carrier USS George Washington (CVN 73). The George Washington Carrier Strike Group is currently participating in Partnership of the Americas, a maritime training and readiness deployment of the U.S. Naval Forces with Caribbean and Latin American countries in support of the U.S. Southern Command objectives for enhanced maritime security. (U.S. Navy photo by Photographer's Mate 3rd Class Robert Brooks)

21 April 2006, Persian Gulf – The Royal Australian Navy frigate HMAS Ballarat (FFH 155) takes on fuel from the Nimitz-class aircraft carrier USS Ronald Reagan (CVN 76). (U.S. Navy photo by Photographer's Mate 3rd Class Aaron Burden)

18 April 2006, Kodiak, Alaska – The Coast Guard Cutter SPAR (WLB 206) returns to the pier after going through its ready for sea trial in Woman's Bay near Coast Guard base Kodiak. The SPAR was named in honor of the 11,000 women who served in the United States Coast Guard during World War II. "Semper Paratus – Always Ready," the Coast Guard motto, was condensed to the S.P.A.R. acronym to symbolize the woman's corps because it reflected their attitude and willingness to contribute to the war effort. (U.S. Coast Guard photo by PA3 Christopher D. McLaughlin)

17 April 2006, South China Sea – The guided-missile cruiser USS Mobile Bay (CG 53), left, and guided-missile destroyer USS Shoup (DDG 86) underway in the Western Pacific. (U.S. Navy photo by Mass Communications Specialist Seaman Justin R. Blake)

25 April 2006, Mayport, Florida – A Coast Guard crew from Station Mayport conduct training in the a 47-foot motor life boat off the coast of Atlantic Beach, Florida. (U.S. Coast Guard photo by PA1 Donnie Brzuska)

26 April 2006, Newport News, Virginia – The propellers of the Pre-Commissioning Unit (PCU) George H.W. Bush (CVN 77) are installed at the Northrop Grumman Newport News shipyard. (Photo by Mr. John Whalen courtesy Northrop Grumman Ship Building)

28 April 2006, Persian Gulf – A landing craft air cushion vehicle (LCAC-72), assigned to ACU-5 prepares to enter the well deck aboard amphibious assault ship USS Peleliu (LHA 5). (U.S. Navy photo by Lithographer 3rd Class Cody D. Lund)

1 May 2006, Port Everglades, Florida – The nuclear-powered fast-attack submarine USS Hampton (SSN 767) arrives in support of South Florida's Fleet Week USA. Nearly 3,000 Sailors participated in this year's event. (U.S. Navy photo by Journalist 2nd Class Christine Hannon)

02 May 2006, Norfolk, Virginia – Sailors man the rail as line handlers wait to get the guided-missile frigate USS Nicholas (FFG 47) underway. Nicholas was deploying as part of the Enterprise Carrier Strike Group. (U.S. Navy photo by Journalist 2nd Class Joshua Glassburn)

5 May 2006, Persian Gulf –
The guided missile destroyer
USS McCampbell (DDG 85)
comes alongside the Nimitz-
class aircraft carrier USS
Ronald Reagan (CVN 76) for
a routine fueling at sea.
Reagan and embarked
Carrier Air Wing One Four
(CVW-14) are currently
deployed as part of a rou-
tine rotation of U.S. mar-
itime forces in the region.
(U.S. Navy photo by
Photographer's Mate 1st
Class James Thierry)

U.S. Naval Vessels

05 May 2006, Pearl Harbor, Hawaii – The guided-missile destroyer USS Hopper (DDG 70) departs Pearl Harbor for a four-month cruise to the U.S. Navy's 7th Fleet area of operations. Hopper will travel to various locations in the Western Pacific to take part in the Cooperation Afloat Readiness and Training (CARAT) 2006 exercise. CARAT is a regularly sched-uled series of military train-ing exercises with Singapore, Thailand, Malaysia, Brunei, and the Philippines designed to enhance interoperability of the respective sea services. (U.S. Navy photo by Chief Journalist Joe Kane)

04 May 2006, Yokosuka, Japan – The guided-missile destroyer USS Stethem (DDG 63) prepares to tow the guided-missile destroyer USS Curtis Wilbur (DDG 54) during a towing exercise that allows a ship to employ a seldom-used, complex procedure for towing ships that are in need of assistance. Multi-Sail is an exercise that allows ships in the Forward Deployed Naval Force to maximize their combat readiness level by participating in maneuvering exercises in a multi-ship environment. (U.S. Navy photo by Ensign Danny Ewing Jr.)

05 May 2006, Pearl Harbor, Hawaii – The guided-missile frigate USS Crommelin (FFG 37) departs for the Western Pacific to take part in the Cooperation Afloat Readiness and Training 2006 exercise. The Crommelin is the 28th ship of the Oliver Hazard Perry-class of guided-missile frigates, was named for the only five brothers ever to graduate from the U.S. Naval Academy (U.S. Navy photo by Chief Journalist Joe Kane)

07 May 2006, Atlantic Ocean – The guided-missile frigate USS Nicholas (FFG 47) sails in formation with the Enterprise Carrier Strike Group. The Nicholas, an Oliver Hazard Perry-class frigate, is the third ship to be named for Major Samuel Nicholas, the first commanding officer of the United States Marines. (U.S. Navy photo by Photographer's Mate 3rd Class Joshua Kinter)

07 May 2006, Atlantic Ocean – The USNS Supply (T-AOE 6) sails through the Atlantic Ocean in formation with the Enterprise Carrier Strike Group. USNS Supply is one of Military Sealift Command's four fast combat support ships and is part of the 39 ships in the Naval Fleet Auxiliary Force. The fast combat support ship (AOE) is the largest combat logistics ship. (U.S. Navy photo by Photographer's Mate 3rd Class Joshua Kinter)

U.S. Naval Vessels

10 May 2006, Pacific Ocean – The Military Sealift Command (MSC) hospital ship USNS Mercy (T-AH 19) performs an underway replenishment operation with oiler USNS Pecos (T-AO 197). Mercy is conducting a five-month humanitarian deployment to Southeast Asia and the Pacific Islands. The medical crew aboard Mercy will provide general and ophthalmology surgery, basic medical evaluation and treatment, preventive medicine treatment, dental screenings and treatment, optometry screenings, eyewear distribution, public health training and veterinary services as requested by the host nations. Mercy is uniquely capable of supporting medical and humanitarian assistance needs and is configured with special medical equipment and a robust multi-specialized medical team who can provide a range of services ashore as well as aboard the ship. The medical staff is augmented with an assistance crew, many of whom are from non-governmental organizations that have significant medical capabilities. (U.S. Navy photo by Chief Photographer's Mate Edward G. Martens)

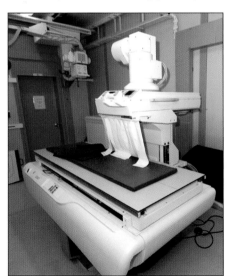

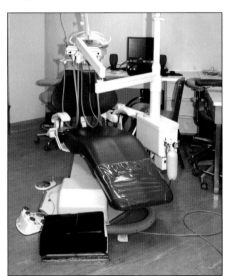

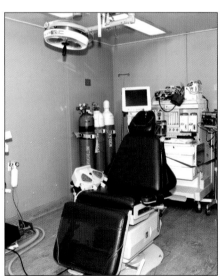

10 May 2006, Pacific Ocean – The hospital ship Mercy (T-AH 19) is fully equipped, including numerous X-Ray machines. (U.S. Navy photo by Journalist Seaman Apprentice Mike Leporati)

10 May 2006, Pacific Ocean – This shows one of the four dental chairs where routine dental work can be done. (U.S. Navy photo by Photographer's Mate 2nd Class Erika N. Jones)

10 May 2006, Pacific Ocean – The Mercy is equipped with two dental surgery rooms that can also be used as regular operating rooms. (U.S. Navy photo by Photographer's Mate 2nd Class Erika N. Jones)

15 May 2006 Pensacola, Florida – The decommissioned aircraft carrier USS Oriskany (CVA 34) is towed out to sea one final time. On 17 May the ship was scuttled 24 miles south of Pensacola in approximately 212 feet of water, becoming the largest ship ever intentionally sunk as an artificial reef. After the Oriskany reaches the bottom, ownership of the vessel will transfer from the Navy to the State of Florida. The public will be allowed to fish and dive on the "Big O" two days later. The keel of this Essex-class carrier was laid in the Brooklyn Naval Shipyard on 1 May 1944, and the 32,000-ton, 888-foot-long carrier was launched on 13 October 1945. However, World War II was over and Oriskany wasn't commissioned until 25 September 1950, and she served proudly in both the Korean and Vietnam conflicts. Oriskany was decommissioned in September 1976 and stricken from the Naval Vessel Register in 1989. (U.S. Navy photo by Photographer's Mate 2nd Jeffrey P. Kraus)

17 May 2006, Newport News, Virginia – The Pre-Commissioning Unit (PCU) Texas (SSN 775) sails into the Northrop Grumman Newport News shipyards with assistance of three tugboats after successfully completing its alpha sea trials. Texas is the second Virginia-class submarine, the first major U.S. Navy combatant class designed with the post-Cold War security environment in mind. (U.S. Navy photo by Photographer's Mate Airman Apprentice Patrick Gearhiser)

17 May 2006, Atlantic Ocean – Lt. Cmdr. Sam Adams stands Officer of the Deck watch from the bridge of the guided-missile submarine USS Florida (SSGN 728). The SSGNs, converted from retired Ohio-class ballistic missile submarines, will be flexible war fighting platforms with capabilities for joint war fighting, including Special Operations Forces and large-scale strike capabilities. The SSGNs (shown in artist concept at left) are equipped with 154 Tomahawk cruise missiles, accommodation for 66 Navy SEALs, and an Advanced SEAL Delivery System (ASDS) mini-sub. (U.S. Navy photo by Chief Journalist Kevin Elliott)

17 May 2006, Atlantic Ocean – Members of the media film inside a lock-out chamber aboard the Ohio-class guided-missile submarine USS Florida (SSGN 728). USS Florida will be officially welcomed to her new home in Kings Bay with a return to service ceremony scheduled for 25 May 2006 in Mayport, Florida. (U.S. Navy photo by Chief Journalist Kevin Elliott)

17 May 2006, Atlantic Ocean – Senior Chief Electronics Technician Andrew Mochrie, seated center, mans the diving officer of the watch in the control room aboard the USS Florida (SSGN 728). Florida is the second of four SSBN submarines to be converted to the guided missile SSGN platform. (U.S. Navy photo by Chief Journalist Kevin Elliott)

24 May 2006, New York Harbor – Sailors spell out the message "I Love New York," on the flight deck aboard the amphibious assault ship USS Kearsarge (LHD 3), as the ship enters the New York Harbor during Fleet Week 2006. Fleet Week has been sponsored by New York City since 1984 in celebration of the United States sea service. The annual event also provides an opportunity for citizens of New York City and the surrounding Tri-State area to meet Sailors, and Marines, as well as witness first hand the latest capabilities of today's Navy and Marine Corps team. Fleet week includes dozens of military demonstrations and displays, including public tours of many of the participating ships. (U.S. Navy photo by Mass Communications Specialist 1st Class Aaron Glover)

19 May 2006, San Diego, California – The amphibious dock landing ship USS Pearl Harbor (LSD 52), sits on blocks in dry-dock prior to its return to sea, following a scheduled repair cycle. Pearl Harbor supports amphibious operations with Air Cushion Landing Craft (LCAC), conventional landing craft, and helicopters. (U.S. Navy photo by Photographer's Mate Airman Joshua Martin)

20 May 2006, White Beach, Okinawa – The Coast Guard Cutter Sherman (WHEC 720) begins its participation in exercise Southeast Asia Cooperation Against Terrorism (SEACAT) 2006 designed to provide participating navies with practical maritime interception training opportunities. USCGC Sherman is home-ported in Alameda, California. (U.S. Navy photo by Senior Chief Journalist Melinda Larson)

U.S. Naval Vessels

25 May 2006, Norfolk, Virginia – *The guided-missile cruiser USS Monterey (CG 61) returns after a two-month deployment. The ship is part of the George Washington Carrier Strike Group, which participated in Partnership of Americas, a maritime training and readiness deployment of the U.S. naval forces with Caribbean and Latin American countries in support of the U.S. Southern Command's objectives for enhanced maritime security.* (U.S. Navy photo by Lithographer 3rd Class Emily A. Zamora)

25 May 2006, Yokosuka, Japan – Four Commander Fleet Activities Yokosuka Port Operations pusher boats file by the conventionally powered aircraft carrier USS Kitty Hawk (CV 63) as it prepares to moor to the pier following a regularly scheduled underway period. (U.S. Navy photo by Photographer's Mate 1st Class Paul J. Phelps)

26 May 2006, Zamboanga, Republic of the Philippines – Medical teams and crew make their way back to the hospital ship USNS Mercy (T-AH 19) after working at the Zamboanga Medical Center. (U.S. Navy photo by Chief Photographer's Mate Edward G. Martens)

29 May 2006, Suez Canal, Egypt – The aircraft carrier USS Enterprise (CVN 65) passes under the Mubarak Peace Bridge along the ship's transit from the Mediterranean Sea to the Red Sea. (U.S. Navy photo by Photographer's Mate 2nd Class Milosz Reterski)

25 May 2006, Santa Rita, Guam – The nuclear-powered fast-attack submarine USS City of Corpus Christi (SSN 705) sails into Apra Harbor. The City of Corpus Christi is currently home-ported at Naval Base Guam, and is the 18th Los Angeles-class attack submarine. (U.S. Navy photo by Photographer's Mate 2nd Class John F. Looney)

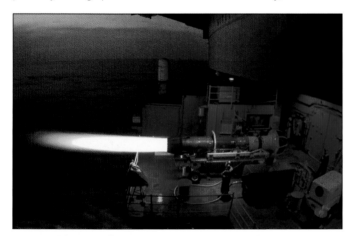

31 May 2006, Pacific Ocean – Aviation intermediate maintenance department jet shop technicians test an F/A-18F Super Hornet jet engine on the fantail aboard the USS Kitty Hawk (CV 63). (U.S. Navy photo by Photographer's Mate Airman Thomas J. Holt)

3 June 2006, Port Klang, Malaysia – USS Ronald Reagan (CVN 76) prepares to enter Port Klang for a scheduled visit, marking the first time Reagan has visited Malaysia. (U.S. Navy photo by Photographer's Mate 2nd Class Aaron Burden)

25 May 2006, South China Sea – Gunner's Mate Seaman Omar Bonilla mans a 25-mm chain gun on the deck of amphibious dock landing ship USS Tortuga (LSD 46) as Gunner's Mate 3rd Class Kevin Rodriguez keeps communication with the bridge during a general quarters drill. (U.S. Navy photo by Photographer's Mate 2nd Class John L. Beeman)

4 June 2006, Mediterranean Sea – The amphibious assault ship USS Saipan (LHA 2) conducts an underway replenishment with USS Simpson (FFG 56) during exercise Phoenix Express 2006. Phoenix Express is a multi-national combined exercise with North African and European forces. (U.S. Navy photo by Photographer's Mate 3rd Class Gary L. Johnson III)

4 June 2006, Mediterranean Sea – A Landing Craft Utility (LCU 1658) assigned to ACU-2 aboard the USS Saipan (LHA 2) crashes through the waves during exercise Phoenix Express. The exercise provides U.S. and allied forces an opportunity to participate in diverse maritime training scenarios. (U.S. Navy photo by Photographer's mate Airman Patrick W. Mullen III)

U.S. Naval Vessels

30 May 2006, South China Sea – The amphibious dock landing ship USS Harpers Ferry (LSD 49) comes alongside the Royal Australian Navy auxiliary oilier replenishment ship HMAS Success (AOR 304), while the amphibious assault ship USS Essex (LHD 2) finishes her underway replenishment. (U.S. Navy photo by Journalist 2nd Class Brian P. Biller)

4 June 2006, Mediterranean Sea – A Landing Craft Utility (LCU 1658) assigned to ACU-2 prepares to enter the well deck of the amphibious assault ship USS Saipan (LHA 2). (U.S. Navy photo by Photographer's mate Airman Patrick W. Mullen III)

6 June 2006, Pacific Ocean – A Sailor stabilizes a RIM-7 Sea Sparrow missile container as it is lowered from the flight deck aboard the Nimitz-class aircraft carrier USS John C. Stennis (CVN 74). (U.S. Navy photo by Photographer's Mate Airman Alan Willis)

06 June 2006, Netherlands Antilles – Landing Craft Utilities (LCU) assigned to ACU-2, rehearse storming the beach in Curacao. ACU-2 is embarked aboard the amphibious assault ship USS Bataan (LHD 5), joining forces from France, Spain, United Kingdom, and Venezuela in the Dutch-led Joint-Caribe Lion 2006 exercise. (U.S. Navy photo by Photographer's Mate 3rd Class Jeremy L. Grisham)

08 June 2006, Jolo, Philippines – The hospital ship USNS Mercy (T-AH 19) assisted thousands of local citizens with medical and dental care working side-by-side with their Filipino counterparts. (U.S. Navy photo by Chief Photographer's Mate Edward G. Martens)

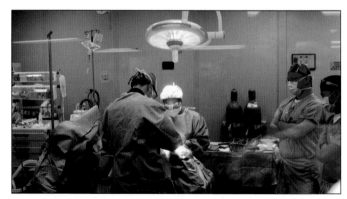

07 June 2006, Jolo, Philippines – A cleft lip operation is performed on a 17-month-old Filipino child aboard the hospital ship USNS Mercy (T-AH 19) by a combination of American and Filipino doctors. (U.S. Navy photo by Chief Photographer's Mate Don Bray)

06 June 2006, Norfolk, Virginia – Sailors man the rails as the amphibious transport dock USS Nashville (LPD 13), an element of the amphibious assault ship USS Iwo Jima Expeditionary Strike group (ESG), departs Naval Station Norfolk on a six-month deployment. (U.S. Navy photo by Lithographer Seaman Apprentice Derek M. Poole)

*08 June 2006, St. Petersburg, Florida – The Coast Guard Cutter Pea Island (WPB 1347), a 110-foot Island-class patrol boat and an Air Station Clearwater HH-60 Jayhawk helicopter, pose in front of the **Sunshine Skyway Bridge**.* (U.S. Coast Guard photo by PA1 Tasha Tully)

09 June 2006, Portland Oregon – Gunners Mates 2nd Class Brandi Matheny and Jeremy Marco clean the five-inch gun turret aboard the guided-missile destroyer USS Preble (DDG 88). (U.S. Navy photo by Mass Communication Specialist 1st Class Ralph Radford)

07 June 2006, South China Sea – Rescue and salvage ship USS Salvor (ARS 52) operates at sea during the Singapore phase of Cooperation Afloat Readiness and Training (CARAT) 2006. CARAT is an annual series of bilateral maritime training exercises between the U.S. and six Southeast Asia nations designed to build relationships and enhance the operational readiness of the participating forces. (U.S. Navy photo by Mass Communication Specialist 1st Class Kathryn Whittenberger)

07 June 2006, South China Sea – 1st Sgt. Adrian Tay from the Republic of Singapore Navy and Machinist's Mate 3rd Class Scott Gee are lowered into the water from the salvage ship USS Salvor (ARS 52). (U.S. Navy photo by Mass Communication Specialist 1st Class Kathryn Whittenberger)

U.S. Naval Vessels

08 June 2006, Yokosuka, Japan – USS Kitty Hawk (CV 63) prepares to pull out of Truman Bay in Yokosuka for a cruise in the western Pacific Ocean. Kitty Hawk is the Navy's oldest active carrier and the only conventionally powered one remaining in commission. (U.S. Navy photo by Photographer's Mate 3rd Class Jarod R Hodge)

08 June 2006, Portland, Oregon – A Portland fire boat greets the Arleigh Burke-class guided missile destroyer USS Preble (DDG 88) with red, white, and blue water streams as she passes under the Willamette River's Steel Bridge. Preble is one of four U.S. Navy ships visiting Portland for the week long 99th annual Rose Festival celebration. (U.S. Navy photo by Mass Communication Specialist First Class Thomas Brennan)

*10 June 2006, Portland, Oregon – The Guided missile destroyers USS John Paul Jones (DDG 53) and USS Preble (DDG 88) are moored in Portland for the 99th Rose Festival. (*U.S. Navy photo by Photographer's Mate 1st Class Bruce McVicar)

*10 June 2006, Portland Oregon – A patrol torpedo boat (PT 658) sails at the Portland Rose Festival. The boat was saved by volunteers and veterans from the Oregon area who successfully restored the 50-ton World War II motor boat to full operational condition including the armament and three original Packard V-12 engines. (*U.S. Navy photo by Mass Communication Specialist 1st Class Ralph Radford)

*10 June 2006, Boston, Massachusetts – The USS Constitution, "Old Ironsides," gets underway for a turn-around cruise in Boston Harbor. The world's oldest commissioned warship will cruise to Fort Independence on Castle Island where it will fire a 21-gun salute before returning to its berth at the Charlestown Navy Yard. (*U.S. Navy photo by Journalist 1st Class Dave Kaylor)

12 June 2006, Alameda, California – The Coast Guard Cutter Aspen (WLB 208), home-ported at Yerba Buena Island in San Francisco, sits in dry dock during an unplanned visit to repair a small leak in the controllable pitch propeller system. While out of the water, Aspen also had work performed on some of the thrusters, the propeller blades were taken off and repaired, and the hull was repainted. (U.S. Coast Guard photo by Petty Officer 1st Class Alan Haraf)

15 June 2006, South China Sea – Sailors assigned to the mine warfare ship USS Patriot (MCM 7), hoist in a mine shape during operations as part of Western Pacific Mine Countermeasures Exercise in Malaysia. (U.S. Navy photo by Mass Communication Specialist 3rd Class Adam R. Cole)

18 June 2006, Philippine Sea – Three Arleigh Burke-class guided-missile destroyers, the USS McCampbell (DDG 85), USS Lassen (DDG 82), and USS Shoup (DDG 86) steam in formation during a photo exercise as part of Valiant Shield 2006. (U.S. Navy photo by Chief Photographer's Mate Todd P. Cichonowicz)

18 June 2006, Philippine Sea – The aircraft carriers USS Ronald Reagan (CVN 76), USS Kitty Hawk (CV 63), and USS Abraham Lincoln (CVN 72) sail in formation at the start of Exercise Valiant Shield 2006. Valiant Shield 2006 is the largest exercise in recent history. Held in the Guam operating area 19-23 June, the exercise includes 28 naval vessels, nearly 300 aircraft, and approximately 22,000 personnel from the Navy, Air Force, Marine Corps, and Coast Guard. (U.S. Navy photos by Chief Photographer's Mate Spike Call and Chief Photographer's Mate Todd P. Cichonowicz)

21 June 2006, Cleveland, Ohio – The decommissioned Coast Guard Cutter Mackinaw (WAGB 83) sailed on her final voyage from her home port of Cheboygan, Michigan, to a permanent berth at the SS Chief Wawatam dock in Mackinaw City where she will be displayed to the public. (U.S. Coast Guard photo)

22 June 2006, San Diego, California – A Navy diver jumps off the buoy deck aboard the Coast Guard Cutter George Cobb (WLM 564) as part of a drill to recover a missile. (U.S. Coast Guard photo by Public Affairs Specialist 3rd Class Mary Larkin T. Jones)

22 June 2006, Pacific Ocean – An SM-3 missile is launched against an incoming ballistic missile target from the guided missile cruiser USS Shiloh (CG 67) during a joint Missile Defense Agency-U.S. Navy test of the Aegis Ballistic Missile Defense System. (U.S. Navy photo)

23 June 2006, Pearl Harbor, Hawaii – The Australian ship HMAS Stuart (FFH 153) pulls into Pearl harbor for a scheduled port call before starting Rim of the Pacific (RIMPAC) 2006. Eight nations are participating in RIMPAC, the world's largest biennial maritime exercise. Conducted in the waters off Hawaii, RIMPAC brings together military forces from Australia, Canada, Chile, Peru, Japan, the Republic of Korea, the United Kingdom, and the United States. (U.S. Navy photo by Photographer's Mate 2nd Class Jason Swink)

23 June 2006, Pearl Harbor, Hawaii – The Peruvian Navy ship BAP Mariatagui (FM 54) pulls into Pearl Harbor for a scheduled port call before starting RIMPAC 2006. (U.S. Navy photo by Photographer's Mate 2nd Class Jason Swink)

23 June 2006, Pearl Harbor, Hawaii – The Japanese Maritime Self Defense Force ship JDS Ariake (DD 109) pulls into Pearl Harbor for a scheduled port call before starting RIMPAC 2006. (U.S. Navy photo by Photographer's Mate 1st Class Dennis C. Cantrell)

23 June 2006, Pearl Harbor, Hawaii – The Chilean Navy training ship TS Esmeralda (BE 43) pulls into Pearl Harbor for a scheduled port call before starting RIMPAC 2006. (U.S. Navy photo by Photographer's Mate 1st Class Dennis C. Cantrell)

23 June 2006, Pearl Harbor, Hawaii – The Chilean Navy ship CS Blanco (FF 15) pulls into Pearl Harbor for a scheduled port call before starting RIMPAC 2006. (U.S. Navy photo by Photographer's Mate 2nd Class Jason Swink)

23 June 2006, Pacific Ocean – Fire controlmen guide a RIM-7 NATO Sea Sparrow missile on its decent to the missile launcher platform during annual maintenance aboard USS Ronald Reagan (CVN 76). (U.S. Navy photo by Photographer's Mate Airman Kathleen Gorby)

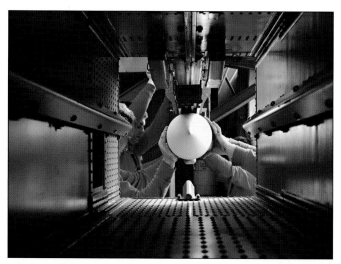

23 June 2006, Pacific Ocean – Fire controlmen aboard the aircraft carrier USS Ronald Reagan (CVN 76) steady a RIM-7 NATO Sea Sparrow missile as it is driven out of its cell for maintenance. (U.S. Navy photo by Photographer's Mate Airman Kathleen Gorby)

23 June 2006, Pacific Ocean – The Nimitz-class aircraft carrier USS John C. Stennis (CVN 74) steams though the calm waters of the Pacific Ocean during routine flight operations. (U.S. Navy photo by Photographer's Mate 3rd Class Ron Reeves)

01 July 2006, Otaru, Japan – USS Kitty Hawk (CV 63) prepares to pull into Otaru, Japan for a port of call following the completion of joint exercise Valiant Shield 2006. (U.S. Navy photo by Mass Communications Specialist 3rd Class Jarod Hodge)

28 June 2006, South Padre Island, Texas – The new Coast Guard 33-foot special purpose law enforcement boats have a top speed of more than 50 knots and are intended to enhance law enforcement capabilities. (U.S. Coast Guard photo by PA2 Adam Eggers)

29 June 2006, Souda Bay, Crete, Greece – Crewmembers aboard USS Nashville (LPD 13) man a Mk 38 25-mm gun. It is designed to provide close range defense against patrol boats, floating mines, and various targets ashore. (U.S. Navy photo by Paul Farley)

30 June 2006, Newport News, Virginia – A conceptual cutaway illustration of the U.S. Navy's San Antonio-class amphibious transport dock ship (LPD). The amphibious transports are used to transport and land Marines, their equipment, and supplies by embarked air cushion or conventional landing craft or amphibious vehicles, augmented by helicopters or vertical take off and landing aircraft in amphibious assault, special operations, or expeditionary warfare missions. (U.S. Navy Illustration provided courtesy Naval Sea Systems Command)

28 June 2006, Pearl Harbor, Hawaii – The Nimitz-class aircraft carrier USS Ronald Reagan (CVN 76) navigates its way through the narrow strait that make up the inlet to Pearl Harbor for a port visit. (U.S. Navy photo by Photographer's Mate Airman Kathleen Gorby)

28 June 2006, Pearl Harbor, Hawaii – The Los Angeles-class fast-attack submarine USS Louisville (SSN 724) returns to her home port after completing a scheduled two month deployment. (U.S. Navy photo by Photographer's Mate 3rd Class Ben A. Gonzales)

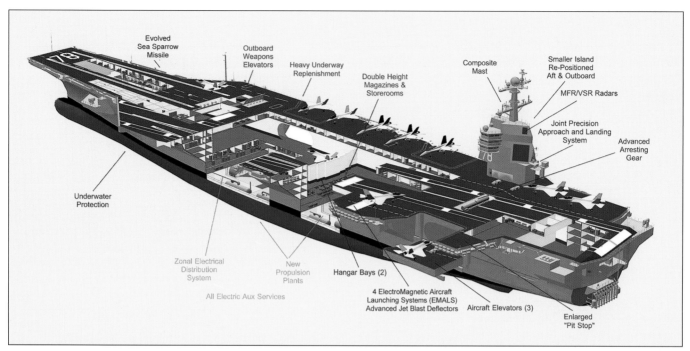

Evolved Sea Sparrow Missile

Outboard Weapons Elevators

Heavy Underway Replenishment

Double Height Magazines & Storerooms

Composite Mast

Smaller Island Re-Positioned Aft & Outboard

MFR/VSR Radars

Joint Precision Approach and Landing System

Advanced Arresting Gear

Underwater Protection

Zonal Electrical Distribution System

New Propulsion Plants

All Electric Aux Services

Hangar Bays (2)

4 ElectroMagnetic Aircraft Launching Systems (EMALS) Advanced Jet Blast Deflectors

Aircraft Elevators (3)

Enlarged "Pit Stop"

30 June 2006, Newport News, Virginia – A conceptual artist's rendering of CVN 78, the first of a new generation carrier design underway at Northrop Grumman Newport News. Construction is slated to begin in 2007. Innovations for the next-generation aircraft carrier include an enhanced flight deck with increased sortie rates, improved weapons movement, a redesigned island, a new nuclear powerplant and allowance for future technologies and reduced manning. (U.S. Navy illustration courtesy Northrop Grumman Newport News Shipbuilding)

30 June 2006, Newport News, Virginia – A conceptual artist's rendering of CVN 78 showing a combination of Boeing F/A-18 Hornets and Lockheed Martin F-35 Lightning IIs on the flight deck. (U.S. Navy Photo courtesy Northrop Grumman Newport News Shipbuilding)

30 June 2006, Pacific Ocean – In preparation for taking on fuel from the USNS John Ericsson (T-AO 194), a pair of gunner's mates fire a shot line from USS Ronald Reagan (CVN 76) to Ericsson. (U.S. Navy photo by Photographer's Mate 2nd Class Aaron Burden)

03 July 2006, Pacific Ocean – The guided-missile destroyer USS Decatur (DDG 73) displays its maneuverability while making a hairpin turn near the aircraft carrier USS Ronald Reagan (CVN 76). (U.S. Navy photo by Mass Communication Specialist Seaman Gary Prill)

04 July 2006, Ho Chi Minh City, Vietnam – Rescue and salvage ship USS Salvor (ARS 52) in holiday dress for a 4th of July celebration. Visits to Vietnam by U.S. Navy ships symbolize the normalization of relations between the two nations. Sailors from Salvor and the mine countermeasures ship USS Patriot (MCM 7) will have an opportunity to interact with the Vietnamese people through a variety of events. (U.S. Navy photo by Mass Communication Specialist 2nd Class John L. Beeman)

06 July 2006, Pacific Ocean – Sailors assigned to the Air Department aboard the Nimitz-class aircraft carrier USS John C. Stennis (CVN 74) conduct a flight deck scrub immediately following the Carrier Air Wing Nine (CVW-9) fly off. (U.S. Navy photo by Mass Communication Specialist 3rd Class Paul Perkins)

04 July 2006, Suez Canal – The amphibious assault ship USS Iwo Jima (LHD 7) transits through the Suez Canal during a scheduled six month deployment. The multi-purpose amphibious assault ship is the flag ship for her Expeditionary Strike Group deployed in support of maritime security operations. Note the variety of Marine Corps and Navy helicopters, including Sikorsky CH-53, Sikorsky HH-60, and Boeing CH-46 types. Also note the NATO Sea Sparrow launcher at the far right of the lower photo. The top photo was taken from one of the deck-edge aircraft elevators. USS Iwo Jima is the seventh Wasp-class amphibious assault ship and the second ship in the Navy to bear the name. The Iwo Jima is also the Navy's third Amphibious Assault Ship designed and built from the keel up with accommodations for female Sailors. (U.S. Navy photos by Mass Communication Specialist 3rd Class Amanda M. Williams and Mass Communication Specialist Airman Joshua T. Rodriguez)

06 July 2006, Pacific Ocean – The guided-missile destroyer USS O'Kane (DDG 77) makes its wake through the Pacific waters near Hawaii during RIMPAC 2006. (U.S. Navy photo by Mass Communication Specialist 3rd Class Marcos T. Hernandez)

05 July 2006, Pearl Harbor, Hawaii – Tugboats assist HMCS Vancouver (FFH 331) in departing from Pearl Harbor to participate in exercise RIMPAC 2006. (U.S. Navy photo by Mass Communication Specialist 2nd Class Rebecca J. Moat)

05 July 2006, Pearl Harbor , Hawaii – The Nimitz-class aircraft carrier USS Abraham Lincoln (CVN 72) departs from Pearl Harbor, Hawaii to participate in exercise RIMPAC 2006. (U.S. Navy photo by Mass Communication Specialist 2nd Class Rebecca J. Moat)

06 July 2006, Coronado, California – Tugboats assist the USS Ronald Reagan (CVN 76) to moor at NAS North Island after completing its maiden deployment. The USS Nimitz (CVN 68) is in the background. (U.S. Navy photo by Chief Mass Communication Specialist Spike Call)

06 July 2006, Pearl Harbor, Hawaii – The Chilean frigate CS Blanco (FF 15) departs from Pearl Harbor to participate in exercise RIMPAC 2006. (U.S. Navy photo by Mass Communication Specialist 2nd Class Rebecca J. Moat)

06 July 2006, Coronado, California – The aircraft carrier USS Ronald Reagan (CVN 76) passes her older sister, the USS Nimitz (CVN 68), on her way home from her first cruise. (U.S. Navy photo by Chief Mass Communication Specialist Spike Call)

05 July 2006, Pearl Harbor, Hawaii – The guided-missile cruiser USS Mobile Bay (CG 53) departs Pearl Harbor to participate in exercise RIMPAC 2006. In the background, the battleship USS Missouri (BB 63) is moored at Ford Island as a memorial. (U.S. Navy photo by Mass Communication Specialist 2nd Class Rebecca J. Moat)

07 July 2006, Pacific Ocean – An SM-2 surface-to-air missile is fired from the aft Vertical Launch System (VLS) aboard the guided-missile destroyer USS O'Kane (DDG 77). (U.S. Navy photo by Mass Communications Specialist Third Class Marcos T. Hernandez)

06 July 2006, Pearl Harbor, Hawaii – The Peruvian Navy ship BAP Mariatagui (FM 54) departs from Pearl Harbor to participate in exercise RIMPAC 2006. (U.S. Navy photo by Mass Communication Specialist 2nd Class Rebecca)

06 July 2006, Pearl Harbor – A U.S. Navy helicopter brings last minute visitors to the Chilean ship CS Blanco (FF 15) as she departs from Naval Station Pearl Harbor for RIMPAC 2006. (U.S. Navy photo by Mass Communication Specialist 2nd Class Brandon A. Teeples)

09 July 2006, Pacific Ocean – Material on the flight deck of the USS Kitty Hawk (CV 63) during a vertical replenishment with the combat stores ship USNS San Jose (T-AFS 7). (U.S. Navy photo by Mass Communication Specialist 3rd Class Jared Benner)

09 July 2006, Indian Ocean – The Arleigh Burke-class guided missile destroyer USS Hopper (DDG 70) pulls alongside the aircraft carrier USS Enterprise (CVN 65) prior to a refueling at sea. (U.S. Navy photo by Mass Communication Specialist 2nd Class Milosz Reterski)

08 July 2006, Newport News, Virginia – The completion of the last of 162 super-lift evolutions scheduled during the construction of the tenth and last Nimitz-class aircraft carrier, George H.W. Bush (CVN 77). The lift placed the ship's 700-ton island superstructure in position on the flight deck. George H. W. Bush is scheduled for christening on 7 October 2006 with delivery to the U.S. Navy in 2008. (U.S. Navy photo courtesy of Northrop Grumman Ship Building)

11 July 2006, Kauai, Hawaii – A landing craft air cushion (LCAC) vehicle assigned to ACU-5 approaches for docking aboard the amphibious assault ship USS Bonhomme Richard (LHD 6), while participating in RIMPAC 2006. (U.S. Navy photo by Mass Communication Specialist Seaman Daniel Taylor)

12 July 2006, Pacific Ocean – The amphibious assault ship USS Bonhomme Richard (LHD 6) evacuates civilians during a simulated non-combatant evacuation operation as part of RIMPAC 2006. (U.S. Navy photo by Mass Communication Specialist Seaman Daniel Taylor)

14 July 2006, Pacific Ocean – USS Dolphin (AGSS 555) Commanding Officer, Cmdr. Andrew Wilde, Culinary Specialist 2nd Class Mark Mundwiller, and Electrician's Mate 1st Class David Carlisle, man the bridge as the Navy's only diesel-electric submarine pulls into her home port at Naval Space and Warfare Systems Command in San Diego. (U.S. Navy photo by Mass Communication Specialist 2nd Class Woody Paschall)

17 July 2006, Souda Bay, Crete, Greece – The guided-missile destroyer USS Gonzalez (DDG 66) gets underway following a brief port visit to Souda Bay. Gonzalez has been assigned escort duties in support of the evacuation of U.S. citizens out of Lebanon. The United States Central Command and U.S. Marines are assisting with the authorized departure of U.S. citizens from Lebanon. (U.S. Navy photo by Mr. Paul Farley)

15 July 2006, Java Sea – The Indonesian frigate KRI Karel Satsuit Tubin (KST 356) operates with Coast Guard Cutter Sherman (WHEC 720) during a maneuvering event as part of the at-sea phase of exercise Cooperation Afloat Readiness and Training. (U.S. Navy photo by Senior Chief Mass Communication Specialist Melinda Larson)

15 July 2006, Strait of Madura – The rescue and salvage ship USS Salvor (ARS 52) at anchor off the coast of Indonesia to conduct dives with Indonesian Navy divers as part of the third phase of exercise Cooperation Afloat Readiness and Training. (U.S. Navy photo by Mass Communication Specialist 2nd Class John L. Beeman)

18 July 2006, Central Command Area of Operations – The amphibious assault ship USS Iwo Jima (LHD 7) sits pierside while loading Marines from the 24th Marine Expeditionary Unit (MEU). Iwo Jima was recently directed to assist in the departure of U.S. citizens from Lebanon. (U.S. Navy photo by Mass Communication Specialist 1st Class Robert J. Fluegel)

19 July 2006, Pacific Ocean – Naval Reserve Officers' Training Corps (NROTC) midshipmen embark the Ohio-class submarine USS Alaska (SSBN 732) for a 24-hour underway guided tour to help familiarize midshipmen with the operations and mission of the submarine community. (U.S. Navy photo by Mass Communication Specialist Seaman Joshua Martin)

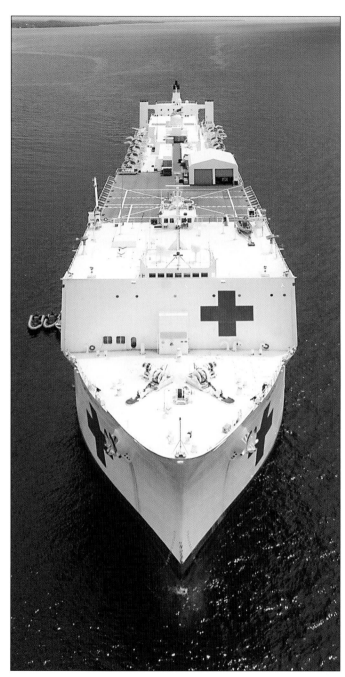

18 July 2006, Nias Island, Indonesia – The hospital ship USNS Mercy (T-AH 19) anchored off the coast of Gunungsitoli City to provide humanitarian and civic assistance. (U.S. Navy photo by Chief Mass Communication Specialist Edward G. Martens)

23 July 2006, off the coast of California – The USS Boxer (LHD 4) conducted a Composite Training Unit Exercise to prepare the strike group for a six-month Western Pacific deployment. (U.S. Navy photo by Mass Communication Specialist 3rd Class Noel Danseco)

19 July 2006, Java Sea – Gunner's Mate 3rd Class Aaron Prenger watches as a fuel probe from the underway replenishment oilier USNS Yukon (T-AO 202) is brought over to rescue and salvage ship USS Salvor (ARS 52) during a refueling at sea. (U.S. Navy photo by Mass Communication Specialist 2nd Class John L. Beeman)

22 July 2006, Bellows AFS, Hawaii – A landing craft air cushion (LCAC) vehicle assigned to ACU-5 embarked on the amphibious assault ship USS Bonhomme Richard (LHD 6) departs from Bellows Beach on the island of Oahu. (U.S. Navy photo by Mass Communication Specialist Seaman Apprentice Jeffrey J. Gabriel Jr.)

20 July 2006, Fairport, Ohio – Members of Coast Guard Station Fairport display the capabilities of 25-foot response boat to Lake Metroparks lifeguards. These boats have a zero to plane time under 4-seconds and a top speed in excess of 40 knots. (U.S. Coast Guard photo by PA2 Matthew Schofield)

22 July 2006, Bellows AFS, Hawaii – A logistical amphibious recovery craft (LARC) disembarks from a landing craft utility (LCU-1646) assigned to Beachmaster Unit One (BMU-1) deployed aboard the USS Bonhomme Richard (LHD 6). (U.S. Navy photo by Mass Communication Specialist 2nd Class Brandon A. Teeples)

24 July 2006, Philippine Sea – The nuclear-powered aircraft carrier USS Enterprise (CVN 65) transits the Philippine Sea while conducting a vertical replenishment with the combat stores ship USNS San Jose (T-AFS 7). (U.S. Navy photo by Mass Communications Specialist Seaman Rob Gaston)

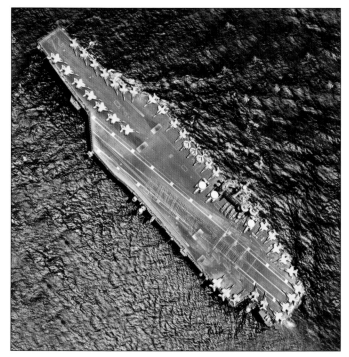

25 July 2006, Pacific Ocean – Sailors aboard the Nimitz-class aircraft carrier USS Abraham Lincoln (CVN 72) spell out "RIMPAC 2006" on the flight deck to commemorate the last day of the world's largest biennial maritime exercise. (U.S. Navy photo by Mass Communication Specialist Seaman James R. Evans)

25 July 2006, Pacific Ocean – The Los Angeles-class fast-attack submarines USS Chicago (SSN 721) and USS Colombia (SSN 771) prepare to join a multinational formation with other ships that participated in the RIMPAC 2006 exercise. (U.S. Navy photo by Mass Communication Specialist Seaman James R. Evans)

25 July 2006, Pacific Ocean – Naval vessels fell into ranks for a photo exercise at the conclusion of RIMPAC 2006. (U.S. Navy photo by Mass Communication Specialist Seaman James R. Evans)

25 July 2006, Pacific Ocean – The guided-missile destroyer USS Milius (DDG 69) sails as part of a 28-ship and 6-submarine formation from the participating nations at the end of RIMPAC 2006. (U.S. Navy photo by Mass Communication Specialist 2nd Class Rebecca J. Moat)

28 July 2006, Atlantic Ocean – The USS Dwight D. Eisenhower (CVN 69) participates in Operation Bold Step, an exercise involving more than 16,000 service members from five countries. (U.S. Navy photo by Mass Communication Specialist 2nd Class Miguel Angel Contreras)

28 July 2006, Atlantic Ocean – An F/A-18F assigned to the "Jolly Rogers" of VFA-103 prepares to launch from the flight deck of the USS Dwight D. Eisenhower (CVN 69). (U.S. Navy photo by Mass Communication Specialist 2nd Class Miguel Angel Contreras)

25 July 2006, Pacific Ocean – The Los Angeles-class nuclear-powered attack submarine USS Key West (SSN 722) sails back to its home port at the conclusion of RIMPAC 2006. (U.S. Navy photo by Mass Communication Specialist 1st Class M. Jeremie Yoder)

28 July 2006, Pacific Ocean – The Coast Guard Cutter Mohawk (WMEC 913) sails in formation in preparation for a gunnery exercise during the UNITAS Pacific Phase exercise. (U.S. Navy photo by Mass Communication Specialist 2nd Class Johansen Laurel)

01 August 2006, St. Petersburg, Florida – Crewmembers from the Aids to Navigation Team maintain a buoy in Tampa Bay with help from a 55-foot Aids to Navigation Boat. Twenty-six 55's were brought into service in 1975 and have live-aboard features so that it can be used in areas where few shore facilities are available. It also has a 4,000-pound cargo capacity and is fitted with a 500-gallon per minute fire pump, Differential Global Positioning System (DGPS) linked to the boat's steering and charting system, both male and female berthing areas, on board sanitary facilities, nd 4-inch icebreaking capabilities. (U.S. Coast Guard photo by PA1 Tasha Tully)

31 July 2006, Miami, Florida – The Coast Guard Cutter Gannet (WPB 87334) patrols past the Port of Miami with the President of the United States and the Commandant of the Coast Guard aboard. (U.S. Coast Guard photo by PA1 Dana Warr)

01 August 2006, Tampa, Florida – A Coast Guard homeland security boat and helicopter with a joint FBI and Coast Guard boarding team simulate intercepting a ship carrying hazardous cargo during Bay Sentinel 2006. (U.S. Coast Guard photo by PA1 Donnie Brzuska)

04 August 2006, Pearl Harbor, Hawaii – The guided-missile destroy-er USS Paul Hamilton (DDG 60) returns to its home port at Pearl Harbor after participating in RIMPAC 2006. (U.S. Navy photo by Chief Mass Communication Specialist Joe Kane)

04 August 2006, San Diego, California – The guided-missile cruiser USS Mobile Bay (CG 53) returns to its home port after completing a regular scheduled deployment. (U.S. Navy photo by Mass Communication Specialist Seaman James Seward)

14 August 2006, Tarakan, Indonesia – The morning sun rises off the bow of the hospital ship USNS Mercy (T-AH 19) in the fourth month of her five-month humanitarian assistance deployment. (U.S. Navy photo by Chief Mass Communication Specialist Edward G. Martens)

14 August 2006, Yokosuka, Japan – Pusher boats pull back into port as tugboats escort the submarine tender USS Frank Cable (AS 40) as it departs after a routine port visit. (U.S. Navy photo by Mass Communication Specialist 1st Class Paul J. Phelps)

16 August 2006, Silverdale, Washington – The Jimmy Carter (SSN 23) is the third and final submarine of the Seawolf-class. A unique feature of the Jimmy Carter is a 100-foot hull extension called the Multi-Mission Platform, which provides enhanced payload capabilities including special forces berthing. (U.S. Navy photo by Master Chief Mass Communication Specialist Jerry McLain)

07 August 2006, Pearl Harbor, Hawaii – The guided-missile cruiser USS Port Royal (CG 73) and amphibious assault ship USS Peleliu (LHA 5) sit moored pierside after completion of a six-month deployment to the Western Pacific. (U.S. Navy photo by Mass Communication Specialist 1st Class James E. Foehl)

10 August 2006, Pascagoula, Mississippi – The Pre-Commissioning Unit (PCU) Makin Island (LHD 8) is the Navy's first amphibious assault ship equipped with all-electric auxiliary systems and a hybrid gas turbine-electric propulsion system. (Photo by Mr. Steve Blount courtesy of Northrop Grumman Ship Building)

U.S. Naval Vessels

16 August 2006, Silverdale, Washington – The Seawolf-class attack submarine USS Jimmy Carter (SSN 23) sits moored in the Magnetic Silencing Facility at Naval Base Kitsap (formerly Naval Submarine Base Bangor) for her first deperming treatment to reduce her electromagnetic signature as she travels through the water. (U.S. Navy photo by Master Chief Mass Communication Specialist Jerry McLain)

15 August 2006, Norfolk, Virginia – Tugboats assist the amphibious assault ship USS Saipan (LHA 2) as it departs Naval Station Norfolk. Saipan is departing on a six-month surge deployment in support of the global war on terrorism. (U.S. Navy photo by Mass Communication Specialist 2nd Class Justin K. Thomas)

16 August 2006, Atlantic Ocean – The amphibious transport dock USS San Antonio (LPD 17) fires the ship's Rolling Air Frame Missile launcher for the first time during a live-fire exercise. The RIM-116 is a short-range, infrared anti-aircraft missile. (U.S. Navy photo by Mass Communication Specialist 3rd Class Anthony C. Tornetta)

14 August 2006, Pacific Ocean – While on patrol in the Eastern Pacific Ocean in early August, the guided-missile frigate USS Stephen W. Groves (FFG 29) took down a "go fast" boat loaded with an estimated 2.6 metric tons of cocaine and interdicted another "go fast" that was preparing to load narcotics. Less than two weeks later, the ship and embarked Coast Guard Law Enforcement Detachment (LEDET) 105 interdicted a third "go fast" boat. Stephen W. Groves was able to close to within a few miles of the "go fast" before being detected and having to give chase. Stephen W. Groves pursued the "go fast" at high speed for the next hour and a half before catching her and detaining her four crew members. "It is really rare to capture a fully fuelled 'go-fast' in a flat-out chase," said Lt. j.g. Scott McCann, LEDET 105 officer in charge. "It is estimated this bust prevented 3 metric tons of cocaine from making it to the United States." (U.S. Navy photo)

16 August 2006, Marinette, Wisconsin – The first Littoral Combat Ship, Freedom (LCS 1) is shown under construction. LCS is a new class of ship designed to be a fast, agile and networked warship able to execute focused missions to defeat shallow water threats such as mines, diesel-electric submarines, and fast surface crafts. (U.S. Navy photo courtesy of Lockheed Martin Corporation)

16 August 2006, Avondale, Louisiana – Construction aboard the amphibious transport dock ship Pre-Commissioning Unit (PCU) New York (LPD 21), the fifth ship in the San Antonio-class. The bow stem is made of steel from the World Trade Centers and weighs 7.5 metric tons. New York is scheduled to be commissioned in the fall of 2008. The San Antonio class is replacing the older Austin-, Cleveland-, and Trenton–class LPDs as well as the Anchorage-class dock landing ships, Newport-class tank landing ships, and one class that has already been retired, the Charleston-class amphibious cargo ships. (U.S. photo by Mass Communication Specialist Seaman Santos Huante)

17 August 2006, Onslow Beach, North Carolina – A Marine Corps High Mobility Multi-purpose Wheeled Vehicle (HMMWV) drives aboard a Landing Craft, Air Cushion (LCAC) assigned to ACU-4 enroute to the amphibious assault ship USS Bataan (LHD 5). Bataan is underway conducting an Expeditionary Strike Group Integration with USS Shreveport (LPD 12), USS Oak Hill (LSD 51), and embarked elements of Amphibious Squadron Two and 26th MEU. (U.S. Navy photo by Mass Communication Specialist Third Class Pedro A. Rodriguez)

18 August 2006, Red Sea – The amphibious assault ship USS Iwo Jima (LHD 7) pulls along side the oiler USNS Kanawha (T-AO 196) for an underway replenishment. (U.S. Navy photo by Mass Communication Specialist Seaman Christopher L. Clark)

18 August 2006, Indian Ocean – The conventionally-powered aircraft carrier USS Kitty Hawk (CV 63) prepares to commence cyclic flight operations while operating off the coast of Australia. Currently underway in the 7th Fleet area of responsibility, Kitty Hawk demonstrates power projection and sea control as the U.S. Navy's only permanently forward-deployed aircraft carrier. (U.S. Navy photo by Mass Communication Specialist Seaman Stephen W. Rowe)

17 August 2006, Atlantic Ocean – Amphibious Assault Ship USS Saipan (LHA 2) test fires its 20-mm close-in weapons system (CIWS) while transiting across the Atlantic Ocean. (U.S. Navy photo by Mass communication Specialist Seaman Patrick W. Mullen III)

20 August 2006, Pacific Ocean – Sailors scrub the flight deck of the amphibious assault ship USS Boxer (LHD 4) after testing the ship's Aqueous Film Forming System. (U.S. Navy photo by Mass Communication Specialist Seaman Paul Polach)

20 September 2006, Pearl Harbor, Hawaii – The hospital ship USNS Mercy (T-AH 19) enters Pearl Harbor for a brief port visit before return-
ing to its home port in San Diego, California. Mercy carried volunteers from Project HOPE and Aloha Medical Mission, along with a contin-
gent of military medical specialists from the United States, India, Malaysia, and Canada. The Mercy contains twelve fully equipped operat-
ing rooms, a 1,000-bed hospital facility, digital radiological services, a diagnostic and clinical laboratory, a pharmacy, an optometry lab, a
cat scan and two oxygen-producing plants. The hospital ship is a converted San Clemente-class supertanker. (U.S. Navy photo by Mass
Communication Specialist First Class Dennis C. Cantrell)

*22 August 2006, Red Sea – Operations Specialist 2nd Class Phillip
Montgomery updates a status board on the amphibious transport
dock ship USS Nashville (LPD 13) bridge.* (U.S. Navy photo by Mass
Communication Specialist 1st Class Shonn Moore)

*22 August 2006, Norfolk, Virginia – Personnel stationed aboard the
Pre-Commissioning Unit (PCU) Texas (SSN 775) stand topside as she
heads for her commissioning in Galveston, Texas.* (U.S. Navy photo
by Mass Communication Specialist Seaman Kelvin Edwards)

25 August 2006, Pensacola Bay, Florida – A TH-57 training helicopter from NAS Whiting Field makes a landing aboard the Navy Helicopter Landing Trainer (HLT) IX-514, marking the 100,000th consecutive accident-free landing on the ship. The helicopter was crewed by student pilot Navy Lt. j.g. David Dostal and instructor Navy Lt. Teresa Ferry. (U.S. Navy photo by Gary Nichols)

25 August 2006, Port Canaveral, Florida – The Virginia-class attack submarine USS Texas (SSN 775) is guided into port by local tugboats near Port Canaveral. Texas will be commissioned on 9 September 2006 in Galveston, Texas. (U.S. Navy photo by Mass Communication Specialist 2nd Class Roadell Hickman)

25 August 2006, Port Canaveral, Florida – Officer of the Deck (OOD) Lt. j.g. Darrin Barber, left, heads out to sea aboard the Virginia-class submarine USS Texas (SSN 775) with a group of local and national media. The second boat in her class, Texas is able to attack targets ashore with highly accurate Tomahawk cruise missiles and conduct covert long-term surveillance of land areas, littoral waters, or other naval forces. Other missions include anti-submarine and anti-ship warfare, special forces delivery and support, mine delivery, and minefield mapping. (U.S. Navy photo by Mass Communication Specialist 2nd Class Roadell Hickman)

29 August 2006, Pascagoula, Mississippi – The Coast Guard Cutter Bertholf (WMSL 750) under construction at the Northrop Grumman Ship Systems facility as part of the Deepwater Program. Deepwater is a critical multi-year, multi-billion dollar program to modernize and replace the Coast Guard's aging ships and aircraft, and improve command and control and logistics systems. It is the largest recapitalization effort in the history of the Coast Guard. (U.S. Navy photo courtesy of Gordon Peterson, Northrop Grumman Ship Building)

29 August 2006, Pascagoula, Mississippi – The day after the one-year anniversary of Hurricane Katrina, the propellers were mounted at the Coast Guard Cutter Bertholf (WMSL 750). (U.S. Navy photo courtesy of Gordon Peterson, Northrop Grumman Ship Building)

29 August 2006, Gulf of Aden – Aviation Warfare Systems Operator 3rd Class Kevin C. Marks observes the USS Cole (DDG 67) while conducting flight operations from the USS Iwo Jima (LHA 7). (U.S. Navy photo by Mass Communication Specialist Seaman Christopher L. Clark)

29 August 2006, Gulf of Aden – The guided-missile destroyer USS Cole (DDG 67) underway patrolling the Gulf of Aden as part of the Iwo Jima Expeditionary Strike Group. Cole deployed from her home port of Norfolk, Virginia, beginning a regularly scheduled six-month deployment in support of maritime patrol operations. The Cole had been attacked by terrorists on 12 October 2000 while it was harbored in the Yemeni port of Aden. (U.S. Navy Photo By Mass Communication Specialist Seaman Christopher L. Clark)

29 August 2006, Gulf of Aden – Amphibious assault ships like the USS Iwo Jima (LHD 7) project power and maintain presence by serving as the cornerstone of the Expeditionary Strike Group. These ships transport and land elements of the Marine Expeditionary Brigade with a combination of aircraft and landing craft and provide fire support with AV-8B Harriers and AH-1 Cobras. (U.S. Navy Photo By Mass Communication Specialist Seaman Christopher L. Clark)

29 August 2006, San Diego, California – U.S. Coast Guardsmen assigned to Maritime Safety Security Team 91103 use the Integrated Anti-Swimmer equipment with divers in the water during Exercise Seahawk 2006. The exercise is a combination of anti-terrorism and force protection training involving units from U.S. Navy Expeditionary Combat Command. (U.S. Navy photo by Mass Communication Specialist 2nd Class Jennifer A. Villalovos)

30 August 2006, Atlantic Ocean – Air Department Sailors on the USS George Washington (CVN 73) practice rigging the emergency aircraft barricade during a flight deck drill during training evolutions off the coast of Virginia. (U.S. Navy photo by Mass Communication Specialist Seaman Tanner Lange)

30 August 2006, South China Sea – The underway replenishment ship USNS Tippecanoe (T-AO 199) refuels and re-supplies the aircraft carrier USS Kitty Hawk (CV 63) and the guided-missile destroyer USS Lassen (DDG 82). (U.S. Navy photo by Mass Communication Specialist Seaman Patrick L. Heil)

U.S. Naval Vessels

30 August 2006, San Diego, California – Gunner's Mate Seaman Justin Baker, assigned to Inshore Boat Unit One Three (IBU-13), mans a 7.62-mm M-240 machine gun while conducting fast boat maneuvers during exercise Seahawk 2006. (U.S. Navy photo by Mass Communication Specialist 2nd Class Jennifer A. Villalovos)

31 August 2006, Mediterranean Sea – One of the landing craft, utility (LCU-1658) boats from the amphibious assault ship USS Saipan (LHA 2) practices small boat operations during a routine deployment. (U.S. Navy Photo by Mass Communication Specialist Seaman McKinley Cartwright)

30 August 2006, Galveston, Texas – A 25-foot response boat and crew from Coast Guard Maritime Safety and Security Team Galveston speeds across the water. This full-scale exercise involved boat crews, underwater divers, bomb detection teams, and bomb-sniffing dog. (U.S. Coast Guard photo by PA2 Adam Eggers)

01 September 2006, Boston, Massachusetts – USS Constitution renders a 21-gun salute during the year's second Chief Petty Officer cruise. Each year, Constitution hosts 300 CPO selectees for sail handling, gun drill training, and community outreach. (U.S. Navy photo by Mass Communication Specialist Airman Nick Lyman)

06 September 2006, Gulf of Aden – A landing craft personnel large (LCPL) is lowered over the side of the amphibious assault ship USS Saipan (LHA 2). (U.S. Navy photo by Mass Communication Specialist Seaman McKinley Cartwright)

07 September 2006, Mediterranean Sea – Crew members aboard the multi-purpose amphibious assault ship USS WASP (LHD 1) load RIM-116 rolling airframe missiles (RAM) into a launcher. (U.S. Navy Photo by Mass Communications Specialist 3rd Class Sarah West)

08 September 2006, Norfolk, Virginia – The advanced auxiliary dry cargo/ammunition ship USNS Lewis and Clark (T-AKE 1) prepares to moor at Naval Station Norfolk. Lewis and Clark is the first of the newest class of underway replenishment ships built for naval service and is named in honor of the legendary explorers. Lewis and Clark is the lead ship in the Navy's new 11-ship class intended to replace the current capability of the Kilauea-class (T-AE 26) ammunition ships, Mars-class (T-AFS 1) combat stores ships, and when operating with Henry J. Kaiser-class (T-AO 187) oiler ships, the Sacramento-class (AOE 1) fast combat support ships. (U.S. Navy photo by Mass Communication Specialist Seaman Justan K. Williams)

11 September 2006, Pascagoula, Mississippi – The Coast Guard Cutter Bertholf (WMSL 750) shown two months before its scheduled christening on 11 November 2006. (U.S. Navy photo courtesy of Gordon Peterson, Northrop Grumman Ship Building)

07 September 2006, Arabian Sea – The amphibious assault ship USS Iwo Jima (LHD 7) conducts flight operations in the Arabian Sea during a six-month deployment to the area. (U.S. Navy photo by Mass Communication Specialist Airman Michael Minkler)

06 September 2006, Pearl Harbor, Hawaii – The Chinese Navy oiler Hongzehu (AOR 881) arrived for a routine port visit to allow Chinese Sailors to experience the unique culture of Hawaii. (U.S. Navy photo by Mass Communication Specialist 3rd Class Ben A. Gonzales)

11 September 2006, Pascagoula, Mississippi – American heroes and innocent victims were honored as Northrop Grumman Corporation laid the keel for the second Legend-class U.S. Coast Guard National Security Cutter (NSC), USCGC Waesche (WMSL 751), on the fifth anniversary of the terrorist attacks of 11 September 2001. (U.S. Navy photo courtesy of Northrop Grumman Ship Building)

10 September 2006, Newport News, Virginia – Pre-Commissioning Unit (PCU) George H.W. Bush (CVN 77) shown in dry dock at the Northrop Grumman Newport News shipyard. CVN 77 is the tenth and last Nimitz-class aircraft carrier and is scheduled for christening in October 2006 with delivery to the U.S. Navy in 2008. (U.S. Navy photo by Mr. Chris Oxley courtesy Northrop Grumman Ship Building)

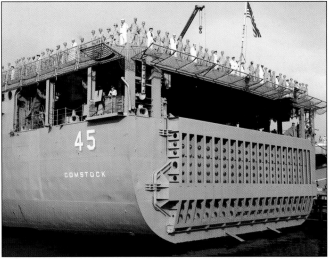

17 September 2006, Arabian Sea – An MH-60S Seahawk assigned to HSC-28 picks up supplies from the fast-combat support ship USNS Supply (T-AOE 6) to unload on the flight deck of the nuclear-powered aircraft carrier USS Enterprise (CVN 65) during a replenishment at sea. (U.S. Navy photo by Mass Communication Specialist Seaman Dale Patrick B. Frost)

13 September 2006, San Diego, California – Sailors and Marines man the rails aboard the amphibious dock landing ship USS Comstock (LSD 45) as the ship departs for a scheduled Western Pacific deployment as part of Expeditionary Strike Group Five. (U.S. Navy photo by Mass Communication Specialist Seaman Michelle Rhonehouse)

U.S. Naval Vessels

18 September 2006, Souda Bay, Crete – (left, above, and below) The Los Angeles-class fast attack submarine USS Dallas (SSN 700) arrives for a port visit. Dallas has a dry deck shelter for Special Operations Forces. (U.S. Navy photo by Mr. Paul Farley)

16 September 2006, Sasebo, Japan – USS Patriot (MCM 7) sits moored at the Ship Repair Facility to avoid damage from the incoming Typhoon Shanshan. (U.S. Navy Photo by Mass Communication Specialist 3rd Class Adam R. Cole)

20 September 2006, Pearl Harbor, Hawaii – The hospital ship USNS Mercy (T-AH 19) passes the USS Arizona Memorial as the ship prepares to moor at Naval Station Pearl Harbor after completing a humanitarian and civic assistance deployment. (U.S. Navy photo by Mass Communication Specialist James E. Foehl)

20 September 2006, Pearl Harbor, Hawaii – A rainbow spans over the Ford Island Bridge as the hospital ship USNS Mercy (T-AH 19) sits moored pierside. The recent deployment saw the ship sail to most of South and Southeast Asia. (U.S. Navy photo by Mass Communication Specialist James E. Foehl)

19 September 2006, Persian Gulf – The amphibious assault ship USS Saipan (LHA 2) and mine countermeasure ship USS Ardent (MCM 12) conduct mine sweeping operations. (U.S. Navy Photo By Mass Communication Specialist 3rd Class Gary L. Johnson III)

20 September 2006, Newport News, Virginia – The Virginia-class nuclear attack submarine North Carolina (SSN 777) under construction at the Northrop Grumman shipyard. (U.S. Navy photo by Mass Communication Specialist Seaman Apprentice Ryan Lee Steinhour)

23 September 2006, Marinette, Wisconsin – The first Littoral Combat Ship, Freedom (LCS 1), the inaugural ship in an entirely new class of U.S. Navy surface warships, is side launched during her christening at the Marinette Marine shipyard. The agile 377-foot-long Freedom was designed and built by a team led by Lockheed Martin. The ship will help the U.S. Navy defeat growing littoral, or close-to-shore, threats and provide access and dominance in coastal water battle-space. Displacing 3,000 metric tons and with a capability of reaching speeds in excess of 40 knots, Freedom will be a fast, maneuverable, and networked surface combatant with operational flexibility to execute focused missions, such as mine warfare, anti-submarine warfare, surface warfare, and humanitarian relief. (Photo released courtesy Lockheed Martin)

30 September 2006, Boston Harbor, Massachusetts – Seventy Medal of Honor recipients get underway aboard USS Constitution, the oldest commissioned ship afloat, for a Medal of Honor flag presentation in Boston Harbor. The Medal of Honor is the United States' highest military honor, awarded for acts of valor above and beyond the call of duty. (U.S. Air Force photo by Janice Abate)

30 September 2006, Boston Harbor, Massachusetts – Vice Chief of Naval Operations (VCNO) Adm. Robert F. Willard arrives aboard USS Constitution. More than 70 Medal of Honor recipients got underway on "Old Ironsides" for the ceremony and presentation of the newly created Medal of Honor Flag. (U.S. Navy photo by Mass Communication Specialist 1st Class Chad J. McNeeley)

U.S. Naval Vessels

21 September 2006, Persian Gulf – A landing craft air cushion (LCAC) leaves the well deck aboard USS Iwo Jima (LHD 7) during a deployment. (U.S. Navy photo by Mass Communication Specialist Seaman Christopher L. Clark)

03 October 2006, Norfolk, Virginia – The Nimitz-class aircraft carrier USS Dwight D. Eisenhower (CVN 69) passes Fort Monroe as it leaves Naval Station Norfolk. (U.S. Navy photo by Mass Communication Specialist 2nd Class Miguel Angel Contreras)

21 September 2006, Norfolk, Virginia – The amphibious transport dock USS Trenton (LPD 14) returns from her last deployment. After 35 years of active service she will be decommissioned and transferred to the Indian Navy in January. (U.S. Navy photo by Mass Communication Specialist 2nd Class Joshua Glassburn)

03 October 2006, Norfolk, Virginia – The guided-missile destroyer USS Mason (DDG 87) gets underway in support of the on-going rotation of forward-deployed forces as part of the Eisenhower Carrier Strike Group. (U.S. Navy photo by Mass Communication Specialist 2nd Class Lolita M. Lewis)

03 October 2006, Norfolk, Virginia – Fast-attack submarines USS Minneapolis-St. Paul (SSN 708) and USS Newport News (SSN 750) prepare to get underway for a scheduled six-month deployment as part of the Eisenhower Carrier Strike Group. Nearly 6,500 Sailors deployed from Norfolk with the Eisenhower CSG in support of the ongoing rotation of forward-deployed forces. (U.S. Navy photo by Mass Communication Specialists 1st Class Christina M. Shaw)

03 October 2006, Norfolk, Virginia – The Los Angeles-class submarine USS Newport News (SSN 750) gets underway. In addition to several small radar units, the sail contains a Type 2 attack periscope (port) and Type 18 search periscope (starboard). (U.S. Navy photo by Mass Communication Specialists 1st Class Christina M. Shaw)

U.S. Naval Vessels

04 October 2006, Portland, Maine – Coast Guard Cutter Marcus Hannah (WLM 554) is fitted with a Vessel of Opportunity Skimming System (VOSS) during an oil spill training exercise in Casco Bay, Maine. The VOSS can be attached to virtually any vessel near an oil spill and is designed to skim oil off the surface of the water and transfer it to an inflatable barge capable of holding 10,000 gallons. (U.S. Coast Guard photo by Petty Officer 3rd Class Lauren Downs)

05 October 2006, Atlantic Ocean – Fire Control Technician 3rd Class Adam Price, Fire Control Technician 1st Class Brian Hassett, and Fire Control Technician 1st Class Clayton Rausch load a Rolling Airframe Missile (RAM) aboard the Nimitz-class aircraft carrier USS Dwight D. Eisenhower (CVN 69). The Mk 49 launcher installation weighs 12,750 pounds and stores 21 RIM-118 missiles. (U.S. Navy photo by Mass Communication Specialist Seaman David Danals)

06 October 2006, Mayport, Florida – Tugboats assist the guided-missile cruiser USS Hue City (CG 66) as she pulls into her home port after completing a surge deployment in support of Maritime Security Operations around the Horn of Africa and relief operations in the Mediterranean Sea. (U.S. Navy photo by Mass Communication Specialist 2nd Class Lynn Friant)

07 October 2006, San Francisco, California – The Coast Guard Cutter Adelie (WPB 87333) and a 25-foot small boat enforce the security zone around the air show over San Francisco Bay for Fleet Week 2006. The air show included performances by the Navy Blue Angels, the Oracle stunt plane, and a SAR demo by a Coast Guard HH-65. (U.S. Coast Guard photo by Petty Officer 3rd Class Kevin J. Neff)

18 October 2006, Persian Gulf – This new Forward Operating Base (FOB) will provide multi-national regional commanders with state-of-the-art command and control features for real-time operations. The base will accommodate Sailors conducting Maritime Security Operations with services such as, food, communications with family and friends, and living quarters while stationed in the Persian Gulf. (U.S. Navy photo by Mass Communication Specialist 2nd Class Justin K. Thomas)

09 October 2006, Pacific Ocean – Sailors aboard guided missile destroyer USS Preble (DDG 88) man the phone and distance line along side the nuclear-powered aircraft carrier USS John C. Stennis (CVN 74) during an underway replenishment. (U.S Navy photo by Mass Communication Specialist 2nd Class Heidi Giacalone)

21 October 2006, Mediterranean Sea – The Nimitz-class aircraft carrier USS Dwight D. Eisenhower (CVN 69) gets underway following a port visit to Naples, Italy. Eisenhower is the flagship for Carrier Strike Group 8. (U.S. Navy Photo by Mass Communication Specialist 2nd Class Miguel Angel Contreras)

19 October 2006, Sata Rita, Guam – The nuclear-powered fast-attack submarine USS Seawolf (SSN 21) enters Apra Harbor. This was the first time a Seawolf-class vessel has made a port call in Guam. The Seawolf-class was the intended successor to the Los Angeles-class, ordered at the end of the Cold War in 1989. At one time, a fleet of 29 submarines was expected to be built over a ten-year period, but this was subsequently reduced to only three boats. (U.S. Navy photo by Mass Communication Specialist 2nd Class Edward N. Vasquez)

23 October 2006, Stennis Space Center, Mississippi – Sailors assigned to Naval Small Craft Instruction and Technical Training School (NAVSCIATTS) train personnel from the Iraqi Riverine Police Force on special boat maneuvers and weapon handling. (U.S. Navy photo by Mass Communication Specialist 1st Class Brien Aho)

24 October 2006, Philippine Sea – The amphibious assault Ship USS Essex (LHD 2) performs a replenishment at sea with the combat stores ship USNS Concord (T-AFS 5) off the coast of the Philippines while participating in the bilateral Exercise Talon Vision. (U.S. Navy photo by Ensign Danny Ewing Jr.)

26 October 2006, Tivat, Montenegro – The Montenegrin ship Jadron sails alongside the guided missile cruiser USS Anzio (CG 68) following a three-day visit by the U.S. Navy ship to strengthen the relationship between the two countries. (U.S. Navy photo by Mass Communication Specialist 3rd Class Matthew D. Leistikow)

24 October 2006, Norfolk, Virginia – The nuclear-powered research submarine, NR-1, docks alongside the submarine support ship M/V Carolyn Chouest. NR-1 is the Navy's smallest submarine, performing underwater search and recovery, oceanographic research missions, and installation and maintenance of underwater equipment to a depth of almost half a mile. (U.S. Navy photo by Mass Communication Specialist Seaman Kelvin Edwards)

03 November 2006, Red Sea – Explosive ordnance disposal personnel assigned to Explosive Ordnance Disposal Mobile Unit Six (EODMU-6) conduct special purpose insertion extraction (SPIE) training from an SH-60 helicopter above the Nimitz-class aircraft carrier USS Dwight D. Eisenhower (CVN 69). (U.S. Navy photo by Mass Communication Specialist 2nd Class Miguel Angel Contreras)

30 October 2006, Persian Gulf – A landing craft utility (LCU-1658) performs small boat operations moments after departing the well deck of amphibious assault ship USS Saipan (LHA 2). (U.S. Navy photo by Mass Communication Specialist Seaman Patrick W. Mullen III)

03 November 2006, Red Sea – The USS Dwight D. Eisenhower (CVN 69), foreground, sails alongside the USS Enterprise (CVN 65) to begin its deployment to the U.S. 5th Fleet. (U.S. Navy photo by Mass Communication Specialist Seaman Rob Gaston)

14 November 2006, Pacific Ocean – A group of 18 U.S. and Japanese Maritime Self-Defense Force ships took part in the bilateral Annual Exercise (ANNUALEX) 2006, designed to improve both forces' capabilities in the defense of Japan. Approximately 8,500 U.S. Sailors are taking part aboard 13 ships, submarines, and various shore-based aircraft. About 90 JMSDF ships and 130 aircraft are also participating. Ships taking part in the exercise-ending photo shoot were the aircraft carrier USS Kitty Hawk (CV 63), two guided-missile cruisers, two Military Sealift Command oilers, two submarines, seven guided-missile destroyers and four JMSDF destroyers. (U.S. Navy photo by Chief Mass Communication Specialist Todd P. Cichonowicz)

11 November 2006, Pascagoula, Mississippi – Coast Guard Admiral Thad Allen and Meryl Justin Chertoff, wife of DHS Secretary Michael Chertoff, are seen at the christening of the Coast Guard Cutter Bertholf (WMSL 750). (Photo Courtesy of Barry Bahler, DHS)

13 November 2006, Yokosuka, Japan – High Speed Vessel Swift (HSV 2) arrives for a routine port visit. The ship was constructed by the Australian shipbuilder Incat in Hobart, Tasmania. (U.S. Navy photo by Mass Communication Specialist 1st Class Paul J. Phelps)

10 November 2006, Chania, Crete, Greece – Sailors prepare to conduct mooring operations as the guided-missile cruiser USS Philippine Sea (CG-58) arrives in Souda Harbor for a routine port visit. (U.S. Navy photo by Mr. Paul Farley)

10 November 2006, Portsmouth, Virginia – A Norfolk Naval Shipyard crane removes the mast from the island of USS George Washington (CVN 73) during a $300 million overhaul. (U.S. Navy photo by Mass Communication Specialist Seaman Jennifer Apsey)

14 November 2006, Newport News, Virginia – Workers from Northrop Grumman Newport News shipyard install a refurbished rudder on USS Carl Vinson (CVN 70) in dry dock. The rudder project is a major milestone in the aircraft carrier's Refueling Complex Overhaul (RCOH). The RCOH is an extensive yard period that all Nimitz-class aircraft carriers go through near the mid-point of their 50-year life cycle. (U.S. Navy photo by Mass Communication Specialist 2nd Class Tekeshia Affa)

14 November 2006, Pacific Ocean – The Los Angeles-class attack submarine USS Asheville (SSN 758) steams in front of the of the USS Kitty Hawk (CV 63) carrier strike group during a photo op. (U.S. Navy photo by Chief Mass Communication Specialist Todd P. Cichonowicz)

18 November 2006, Norfolk, Virginia – The superstructure of the USS Enterprise (CVN 65) is unique among U.S. aircraft carriers and has evolved considerably since the ship was built. (U.S. Navy photo by Mass Communication Specialist Seaman Ash Severe)

17 November 2006, Riga, Latvia – The guided-missile cruiser USS Monterey (CG 61), flagship for Standing NATO Maritime Group Two, during a port visit to the city in support of the upcoming NATO Summit Riga 2006. SNMG-2 was established as NATO's maritime ready response force. (U.S. Navy photo by Mass Communication Specialist 2nd Class Leonardo Carrillo)

20 November 2006, Pearl Harbor, Hawaii – Boatswain's Mate 2nd Class Veronica Greene (left) hauls in a line from the bow of the Commander, Navy Region Hawaii barge as it gets underway from Merry Point Landing. The barge tour affords official visitors an up-close view of Pearl Harbor. (U.S. Navy photo by Mass Communication Specialist 1st Class James E. Foehl)

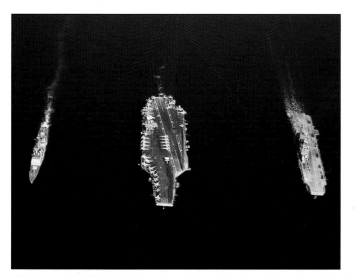

20 November 2006, Arabian Sea – The guided-missile cruiser USS Anzio (CG 68), Nimitz-class aircraft carrier USS Dwight D. Eisenhower (CVN 69), and amphibious assault ship USS Saipan (LHA 2) sail in formation during a photographic exercise. The ships are currently on deployment in the 5th Fleet area of responsibility conducting maritime security operations. (U.S. Navy photo by Mass Communication Specialist Seaman Patrick W. Mullen III)

22 November 2006, South China Sea – The underway replenishment oiler USNS Rappahannock (T-AO 204) prepares to conduct a refueling at sea with USS Kitty Hawk (CV 63). (U.S. Navy photo by Mass Communication Specialist Seaman Thomas J. Holt)

22 November 2006, Persian Gulf – The Military Sealift Command (MSC) fast combat support ship USNS Supply (T-AOE 6), left, conducts an underway replenishment with the dock landing ship USS Comstock (LSD 45). Supply and Comstock are underway in U.S. 5th Fleet's area of operations in support of maritime security operations. (U.S. Navy photo by Mass Communication Specialist 2nd Class Kitt Amaritnant)

21 November 2006, Newport News, Virginia – Workers from Northrop Grumman Newport News shipyard install the port side anchor on the USS Carl Vinson (CVN 70) during the aircraft carrier's Refueling Complex Overhaul. (U.S. Navy photo by Mass Communication Specialist 3rd Class Refugio Carrillo)

21 November 2006, Arabian Sea – Visit, Board, Search and Seizure (VBSS) teams assigned to the amphibious assault ship USS Saipan (LHA 2) crash through the waves aboard a Rigid Hull Inflatable Boat (RHIB) while conducting training in the Arabian Sea. (U.S. Navy photo by Lt. Zach McNeill)

22 November 2006, Persian Gulf – The amphibious assault ship USS Boxer (LHD 4) prepares to come alongside the fast combat support ship USNS Supply (T-AOE 6), for an underway replenishment. Boxer and Supply are underway in U.S. 5th Fleet's area of operations in support of maritime security operations. (U.S. Navy photo by Mass Communication Specialist 2nd Class Kitt Amaritnant)

27 November 2006, Pacific Ocean – The amphibious assault ship USS Bonhomme Richard (LHD 6) fires a Mk 15 Phalanx Close-In Weapons Systems (CIWS). The 20-mm M61 Vulcan gatling gun fires up to 4,500 rounds per minute. (U.S. Navy Photo by Mass Communication Specialist 2nd Class Emmanuel Rios)

27 November 2006, Arabian Sea – A Sailor watches as the Nimitz-class aircraft carrier USS Dwight D. Eisenhower (CVN 69) takes on fuel and other supplies from the underway replenishment oilier USNS Laramie (T-AO 204). (U.S. Navy photo by Mass Communication Specialist Seaman David Danals)

01 December 2006, Manasquan, New Jersey – Station Manasquan Inlet, located in the New Jersey boat basin, is seen here on a clear December day. (U.S. Coast Guard photo by BM1 Kenneth Seebeck)

01 December 2006, Persian Gulf – A Mine Neutralization Vehicle (MNV) is lowered over the side prior to an exercise aboard the mine countermeasures ship USS Ardent (MCM 12). The MNV's mission is to seek and destroy mines. (U.S. Navy photo by Mass Communication Specialist 2nd Class Justin K. Thomas)

02 December 2006, Persian Gulf – Personnel aboard the mine countermeasures ship USS Ardent (MCM 12) move a Type 1 float that is used to conduct mechanical mine sweeping prior to a mine countermeasure exercise. (U.S. Navy photo by Mass Communication Specialist 2nd Class Justin K. Thomas)

04 December 2006, Pearl Harbor, Hawaii – A Sailor assigned to dock landing ship USS Pearl Harbor (LSD 52) adjusts a rat guard on a bow-line. (U.S. Navy photo by Mass Communication Specialist 1st Class James E. Foehl)

04 December 2006, Suez Canal – The amphibious assault ship USS Saipan (LHA 2) transits north through the Suez Canal after successfully completing her last surge deployment before decommissioning in April. (U.S. Navy photo by Mass Communication Specialist Seaman Patrick W. Mullen III)

05 December 2006, North Carolina coast – Sailors assigned to Riverine Squadron One (RIVRON-1) prepare for their final exercise and evaluations near Camp Lejeune, North Carolina, prior to deployment to Southwest Asia. (U.S. Navy photo by Mass Communication Specialist 1st Class Jackey Bratt)

05 December 2006, New York Harbor – A crew aboard a 25-foot Defender-class Response Boat escorts the USS Intrepid as it transits to Bayonne, N.J. The museum ship that is normally moored in New York will undergo a two-year renovation in Bayonne before being towed back to its permanent mooring. Breaking the aircraft carrier loose from the mud where it had been moored was more of a challenge than expected and made the national news for several weeks. (U.S. Coast Guard photo by PA3 Daniel Bender)

07 December 2006, New York – The Coast Guard Cutter Juniper (WLB 201) performs maintenance on a buoy before returning it to sea in the Sandy Hook Channel. The Juniper will be installing new LED lanterns on buoys along the Northeast coast on its winter patrol. (U.S. Coast Guard photo by PA3 Annie R. Berlin)

06 December 2006, Pearl Harbor, Hawaii – The city lights of Aiea, Hawaii, forms the backdrop for USS Arizona Memorial the morning prior to the ceremony commemorating the 65th Anniversary of the attack on Pearl Harbor. (U.S. Navy photo by Mass Communication Specialist 1st Class James E. Foehl)

10 December 2006, Atlantic Ocean – Aboard the aircraft carrier USS Theodore Roosevelt (CVN 71) fire controlmen off-load RIM-7 NATO Sea Sparrow missiles from one of the ship's launchers. (U.S. Navy photo by Mass Communication Specialist 2nd Class Nathan Laird)

06 December 2006, San Diego, California – After officially christening the newest resupply ship, Military Sealift Command (MSC) advanced auxiliary dry cargo/ammunition ship USNS Alan Shepard (T-AKE 3), she is launched into the San Diego Bay during a christening and launching ceremony held at the National Steel and Shipbuilding Company (NASSCO). The Shepard is named after Rear Adm. Alan Bartlett Shepard, who was the first American astronaut in space and the fifth person to walk on the moon. The Shepard is the third of the USNS ships named after great explorers. Its primary mission will be to deliver ammunition, fuel, food, and other supplies to combat ships at sea. (U.S. Navy photo by Mass Communication Specialist 2nd Class Alexis R. Brown)

15 December 2006, Kuwait – After passing a customs inspection, an Army M114 Hummer awaits Navy cargo handlers with NAVELSG Port Group Echo to load it aboard the Military Sealift Command roll-on/roll-off ship USNS Shughart (T-AKR 295). (U.S. Navy photo by Mass Communication Specialist Seaman Kenneth R. Hendrix)

16 December 2006, Portsmouth, Virginia – One of the Advanced Combat Direction System (ACDS) consoles in the Combat Direction Center (CDC) aboard the Nimitz-class aircraft carrier USS Harry S. Truman (CVN 75). (U.S. Navy photo by Mass Communication Specialist 3rd Class Kristopher Wilson)

15 December 2006, Atlantic Ocean – A quartermaster cleans the windows surrounding the command bridge before flight operations aboard the Nimitz-class nuclear-powered aircraft carrier USS Theodore Roosevelt (CVN 71). (U.S. Navy photo by Mass Communication Specialist Seaman Sheldon Rowley)

List of U.S. Navy Ships

The following is an alphabetical list of U.S. Navy ships with their home ports. Please note that ships stationed overseas in Italy and Japan are forward deployed in those ports, not home-ported there. Ships which are named for individuals are listed by the first name of that individual. For example, USS Dwight D. Eisenhower is listed under the "D" rather than the "E." Ships that are USNS are operated with a civilian master and crew by the Military Sealift Command. The absence of "USS" or "no home port" indicates the ship has not been placed in service or has been stricken from active duty and the Naval Register. This was compiled from http://www.navy.mil/navydata/ships/lists/shipalpha.asp on 1 January 2007.

- 1 -

MV 1st Lt. Alex Bonnyman	T-AK 3003	No home port
MV 1st Lt. Baldomero Lopez	T-AK 3010	No home port
USNS 1st Lt. Harry L. Martin	T-AK 3015	No home port
MV 1st Lt. Jack Lummus	T-AK 3011	No home port

- 2 -

MV 2nd Lt. John P. Bobo	T-AK 3008	No home port

- A -

MV A1C William A. Pitsenbarger	T-AK 4638	No home port
USS Abraham Lincoln	CVN 72	Everett, WA
USS Alabama	SSBN 731	Bangor, WA
USS Alaska	SSBN 732	Kings Bay, GA
USS Albany	SSN 753	Norfolk, VA
USS Albuquerque	SSN 706	Portsmouth, NH
USS Alexandria	SSN 757	Groton, CT
USNS Algol	T-AKR 287	No home port
USNS Altair	T-AKR 291	No home port
Anchorage	LPD 23	No home port
USS Annapolis	SSN 760	Groton, CT
USNS Antares	T-AKR 294	No home port
USS Antietam	CG 54	San Diego, CA
USS Anzio	CG 68	Norfolk, VA
USNS Apache	T-ATF 172	No home port
USNS Arctic	T-AOE 8	No home port
USS Ardent	MCM 12	Manama, Bahrain
USS Arleigh Burke	DDG 51	Norfolk, VA
Arlington	LPD 24	No home port
USS Asheville	SSN 758	San Diego, CA
USS Ashland	LSD 48	Little Creek, VA
USS Augusta	SSN 710	Groton, CT
Avalon	DSRV 2	No home port
USS Avenger	MCM 1	Ingleside, TX

- B -

USS Bainbridge	DDG 96	Norfolk, VA
USS Barry	DDG 52	Norfolk, VA
USS Bataan	LHD 5	Norfolk, VA
USNS Beaver State	T-ACS 10	No home port
USNS Bellatrix	T-AKR 288	No home port
USNS Benavidez	T-AKR 306	No home port
USS Benfold	DDG 65	San Diego, CA
USNS Big Horn	T-AO 198	No home port
USS Black Hawk	MHC 58	Ingleside, TX
USS Blue Ridge	LCC 19	Yokosuka, Japan
USNS Bob Hope	T-AKR 300	No home port
USS Boise	SSN 764	Norfolk, VA
USS Bonhomme Richard	LHD 6	San Diego, CA
USS Boone	FFG 28	Mayport, FL
USNS Bowditch	T-AGS 62	No home port
USS Boxer	LHD 4	San Diego, CA
USS Bremerton	SSN 698	Pearl Harbor, HI
USNS Bridge	T-AOE 10	No home port
USNS Brittin	T-AKR 305	No home port
USNS Bruce C. Heezen	T-AGS 64	No home port
USS Buffalo	SSN 715	Pearl Harbor, HI
USS Bulkeley	DDG 84	Norfolk, VA
USS Bunker Hill	CG 52	San Diego, CA

- C -

USNS Capable	T-AGOS 16	No home port
USS Cape St. George	CG 71	Norfolk, VA
USNS Capella	T-AKR 293	No home port
MV Capt. Steven L. Bennett	T-AK 4296	No home port
USS Cardinal	MHC 60	Manama, Bahrain
USS Carl Vinson	CVN 70	Newport News, VA
USS Carney	DDG 64	Mayport, FL
USS Carr	FFG 52	Norfolk, VA
USS Carter Hall	LSD 50	Little Creek, VA
USNS Catawba	T-ATF 168	No home port
USS Chafee	DDG 90	Pearl Harbor, HI
USS Champion	MCM 4	Ingleside, TX
USS Chancellorsville	CG 62	San Diego, California
USS Charlotte	SSN 766	Portsmouth, NH
USNS Charlton	T-AKR 314	No home port
SS Chesapeake	T-AOT 5084	No home port
USS Cheyenne	SSN 773	Pearl Harbor, HI
USS Chicago	SSN 721	Pearl Harbor, HI
USS Chief	MCM 14	Ingleside, TX
USS Chinook	PC 9	Little Creek, VA
USS Chosin	CG 65	Pearl Harbor, HI
USS Chung-Hoon	DDG 93	San Diego, CA
USS City of Corpus Christi	SSN 705	Guam
USS Cole	DDG 67	Norfolk, VA
USS Columbia	SSN 771	Pearl Harbor, HI
USS Columbus	SSN 762	Pearl Harbor, HI
USNS Comfort	T-AH 20	No home port
USS Comstock	LSD 45	San Diego, CA
USNS Concord	T-AFS 5	No home port
USS Connecticut	SSN 22	Groton, CT
USS Cormorant	MHC 57	Ingleside, TX
USNS Cornhusker State	T-ACS 6	No home port
USS Coronado	AGF 11	San Diego, CA
USS Cowpens	CG 63	Yokosuka, Japan
MV Cpl. Louis J. Hauge, Jr.	T-AK 3000	No home port
USS Crommelin	FFG 37	Pearl Harbor, HI
USS Curtis Wilbur	DDG 54	Yokosuka, Japan
SS Curtiss	T-AVB 4	No home port
USS Curts	FFG 38	San Diego, CA
Cutthroat	LSV 2	No home port

- D -

USNS Dahl	T-AKR 312	No home port
USS Dallas	SSN 700	Groton, CT
USS De Wert	FFG 45	Mayport, FL
USS Decatur	DDG 73	San Diego, CA
USS Defender	MCM 2	Ingleside, TX
USNS Denebola	T-AKR 289	No home port
USS Devastator	MCM 6	Ingleside, TX
Dewey	DDG 105	No home port
USS Dextrous	MCM 13	Manama, Bahrain
USNS Diamond State	T-ACS 7	No home port
USS Dolphin	AGSS 555	San Diego, CA
USS Donald Cook	DDG 75	Norfolk, VA
USS Doyle	FFG 39	Mayport, FL
USS Dwight D. Eisenhower	CVN 69	Norfolk, VA

- E -

USNS Effective	T-AGOS 21	No home port
USS Elrod	FFG 55	Norfolk, VA
USS Emory S. Land	AS 39	La Maddalena, Italy
USS Enterprise	CVN 65	Norfolk, VA
USNS Equality State	T-ACS 8	No home port
USS Essex	LHD 2	Sasebo, Japan

- F -

USS Farragut	DDG 99	Mayport, FL
USS Firebolt	PC 10	Little Creek, VA
USNS Fisher	T-AKT 301	No home port
USS Fitzgerald	DDG 62	Yokosuka, Japan
USNS Flickertail State	T-ACS 5	No home port
USS Florida	SSGN 728	Bangor, WA
USS Ford	FFG 54	Everett, WA
USS Forrest Sherman	DDG 98	Norfolk, VA
USS Fort McHenry	LSD 43	Sasebo, Japan
USS Frank Cable	AS 40	Guam

- G -

USS Gary	FFG 51	Yokosuka, Japan
USNS Gem State	T-ACS 2	No home port

George H.W. Bush	CVN 77	No home port
USS George Washington	CVN 73	Norfolk, VA
USS Georgia	SSGN 729	Norfolk, VA
USS Germantown	LSD 42	San Diego, CA
USS Gettysburg	CG 64	Mayport, FL
USNS Gilliland	T-AKR 298	No home port
USS Gladiator	MCM 11	Ingleside, TX
USS Gonzalez	DDG 66	Norfolk, VA
USNS Gopher State	T-ACS 4	No home port
USNS Gordon	T-AKR 296	No home port
USNS Grand Canyon State	T-ACS 3	No home port
USS Grapple	ARS 53	Little Creek, VA
USS Grasp	TARS 51	No home port
Green Bay	LPD 20	No home port
USNS Green Mountain State	T-ACS 9	No home port
USS Greeneville	SSN 772	Pearl Harbor, HI
Gridley	DDG 101	No home port
USNS Guadalupe	T-AO 200	No home port
USS Guardian	MCM 5	Sasebo, Japan
USNS Gunnery Sgt. Fred W. Stockham	T-AK 3017	No home port
USS Gunston Hall	LSD 44	Little Creek, VA
MV Gus W. Darnell	T-AOT 1121	No home port

- H -

USS Halsey	DDG 97	San Diego, Calif.
USS Halyburton	FFG 40	Mayport, FL
USS Hampton	SSN 767	Norfolk, VA
USS Harpers Ferry	LSD 49	Sasebo, Japan
USS Harry S. Truman	CVN 75	Norfolk, VA
USS Hartford	SSN 768	Portsmouth, NH
Hawaii	SSN 776	No home port
USS Hawes	FFG 53	Norfolk, VA
USNS Hayes	T-AG 195	No home port
USS Helena	SSN 725	San Diego, CA
USNS Henry J. Kaiser	T-AO 187	No home port
USS Henry M. Jackson	SSBN 730	Bangor, WA
USNS Henson	T-AGS 63	No home port
USS Heron	MHC 52	Ingleside, TX
USS Higgins	DDG 76	San Diego, CA
USS Hopper	DDG 70	Pearl Harbor, HI
USS Houston	SSN 713	Bremerton, WA
USS Howard	DDG 83	San Diego, CA
USS Hue City	CG 66	Mayport, FL
USS Hurricane	PC 3	Little Creek, VA
USS Hyman G. Rickover	SSN 709	Norfolk, VA

- I -

USNS Impeccable	T-AGOS 23	No home port
USNS Indomitable	T-AGOS 7	No home port
USS Ingraham	FFG 61	Everett, WA
USNS Invincible	T-AGM 24	No home port
USS Iwo Jima	LHD 7	Norfolk, VA

- J -

USS Jacksonville	SSN 699	Norfolk, VA
USS James E. Williams	DDG 95	Norfolk, VA
USS Jarrett	FFG 33	San Diego, CA
USS Jefferson City	SSN 759	San Diego, CA
USS Jimmy Carter	SSN 23	Bangor, WA
USS John C. Stennis	CVN 74	Bremerton, WA
USNS John Ericsson	T-AO 194	No home port
USS John F. Kennedy	CV 67	Mayport, FL
USS John L. Hall	FFG 32	Pascagoula, MS
USNS John Lenthall	T-AO 189	No home port
USNS John McDonnell	T-AGS 51	No home port
USS John Paul Jones	DDG 53	San Diego, CA
USS John S. McCain	DDG 56	Yokosuka, Japan

- K -

USNS Kanawha	T-AO 196	No home port
USS Kauffman	FFG 59	Norfolk, VA
USS Kearsarge	LHD 3	Norfolk, VA
USS Kentucky	SSBN 737	Bangor, WA
USS Key West	SSN 722	Pearl Harbor, HI
USNS Keystone State	T-ACS 1	

Kidd	DDG 100	No home port
USS Kingfisher	MHC 56	Ingleside, TX
USS Kitty Hawk	CV 63	Yokosuka, Japan
USS Klakring	FFG 42	Norfolk, VA

- L -

USS La Jolla	SSN 701	Pearl Harbor, HI
USS Laboon	DDG 58	Norfolk, VA
USS Lake Champlain	CG 57	San Diego, CA
USS Lake Erie	CG 70	Pearl Harbor, HI
USNS Lance Cpl. Roy M. Wheat	T-AK 3016	No home port
USNS Laramie	T-AO 203	No home port
USS Lassen	DDG 82	Yokosuka, Japan
USNS Lawrence H. Gianella	T-AOT 1125	No home port
USNS Leroy Grumman	T-AO 195	No home port
Lewis and Clark	T-AKE 1	No home port
USS Leyte Gulf	CG 55	Norfolk, VA
USS Los Angeles	SSN 688	Pearl Harbor, HI
USS Louisiana	SSBN 743	Bangor, WA
USS Louisville	SSN 724	Pearl Harbor, HI
USNS Loyal	T-AGOS 22	No home port

- M -

USS Mahan	DDG 72	Norfolk, VA
USS Maine	SSBN 741	Bangor, WA
MV Maj. Bernard F. Fisher	T-AK 4396	No home port
MV Maj. Stephen W. Pless	T-AK 3007	No home port
Makin Island	LHD 8	No home port
USNS Mary Sears	T-AGS 65	No home port
USS Maryland	SSBN 738	Kings Bay, GA
USS Mason	DDG 87	Norfolk, VA
USS McCampbell	DDG 85	San Diego, CA
USS McClusky	FFG 41	San Diego, CA
USS McFaul	DDG 74	Norfolk, VA
USS McInerney	FFG 8	Mayport, FL
USS Memphis	SSN 691	Groton, CT
USNS Mendonca	T-AKR 303	No home port
USNS Mercy	T-AH 19	No home port
Mesa Verde	LPD 19	No home port
USS Miami	SSN 755	Groton, CT
USS Michigan	SSGN 727	Bangor, WA
USS Milius	DDG 69	San Diego, CA
USS Minneapolis-St. Paul	SSN 708	Norfolk, VA
USS Mitscher	DDG 57	Norfolk, VA
USS Mobile Bay	CG 53	San Diego, CA
USS Momsen	DDG 92	San Diego, CA
USS Monterey	CG 61	Norfolk, VA
USS Montpelier	SSN 765	Norfolk, VA
USS Mount Whitney	LCC 20	Gaeta, Italy
MT Montauk		No home port
USS Mustin	DDG 89	San Diego, CA
Mystic	DSRV 1	No home port

- N -

USS Nassau	LHA 4	Norfolk, VA
USNS Navajo	T-ATF 169	No home port
USS Nebraska	SSBN 739	Bangor, WA
USS Nevada	SSBN 733	Bangor, WA
New Hampshire	SSN 778	No home port
New Mexico	SSN 779	No home port
New Orleans	LPD 18	No home port
New York	LPD 21	No home port
USS Newport News	SSN 750	Norfolk, VA
USNS Niagara Falls	T-AFS 3	No home port
USS Nicholas	FFG 47	Norfolk, VA
USS Nimitz	CVN 68	San Diego, CA
USS Nitze	DDG 94	Norfolk, VA
USS Norfolk	SSN 714	Norfolk, VA
USS Normandy	CG 60	Norfolk, VA
North Carolina	SSN 777	No home port

- O -

USS O'Kane	DDG 77	Pearl Harbor, HI
USS Oak Hill	LSD 51	Little Creek, VA
USNS Observation Island	T-AGM 23	No home port

Ship	Hull	Home Port
USS Ohio	SSGN 726	Bangor, WA
USS Oklahoma City	SSN 723	Norfolk, VA
USS Olympia	SSN 717	Pearl Harbor, HI
USS Oscar Austin	DDG 79	Norfolk, VA

- P -

Ship	Hull	Home Port
USS Pasadena	SSN 752	Pearl Harbor, HI
USNS Pathfinder	T-AGS 60	No home port
USS Patriot	MCM 7	Sasebo, Japan
USNS Patuxent	T-AO 201	No home port
USNS Paul Buck	T-AOT 1122	No home port
USS Paul Hamilton	DDG 60	Pearl Harbor, HI
USS Pearl Harbor	LSD 52	San Diego, CA
USNS Pecos	T-AO 197	No home port
USS Peleliu	LHA 5	San Diego, CA
USS Pelican	MHC 53	Ingleside, TX
USS Pennsylvania	SSBN 735	Bangor, WA
SS Petersburg	T-AOT 5075	No home port
MV PFC Dewayne T. Williams	T-AK 3009	No home port
MV PFC Eugene A. Obregon	T-AK 3006	No home port
MV PFC James Anderson, Jr.	T-AK 3002	No home port
MV PFC William B. Baugh	T-AK 3001	No home port
USS Philadelphia	SSN 690	Groton, CT
USS Philippine Sea	CG 58	Mayport, FL
USNS Pililaau	T-AKR 304	No home port
USS Pinckney	DDG 91	San Diego, CA
USS Pioneer	MCM 9	Ingleside, TX
USS Pittsburgh	SSN 720	Portsmouth, NH
USNS Pollux	T-AKR 290	No home port
USNS Pomeroy	T-AKR 316	No home port
USS Port Royal	CG 73	Pearl Harbor, HI
USS Porter	DDG 78	Norfolk, VA
USS Preble	DDG 88	San Diego, CA
USS Princeton	CG 59	San Diego, CA
USS Providence	SSN 719	Groton, CT
MV Pvt. Franklin J. Phillips	T-AK 3004	No home port

- R -

Ship	Hull	Home Port
USNS Rainer	T-AOE 7	No home port
USS Ramage	DDG 61	Norfolk, VA
USNS Rappahannock	T-AO 204	No home port
USS Raven	MHC 61	Manama, Bahrain
USNS Red Cloud	T-AKR 313	No home port
USNS Regulus	T-AKR 292	No home port
USS Rentz	FFG 46	San Diego, CA
USS Reuben James	FFG 57	Pearl Harbor, HI
USS Rhode Island	SSBN 740	Kings Bay, GA
USNS Richard G. Matthiesen	T-AOT 1124	No home port
USS Robert G. Bradley	FFG 49	Mayport, FL
USS Rodney M. Davis	FFG 60	Everett, WA
USS Ronald Reagan	CVN 76	San Diego, CA
USS Roosevelt	DDG 80	Mayport, FL
USS Ross	DDG 71	Norfolk, VA
USS Rushmore	LSD 47	San Diego, CA
USS Russell	DDG 59	Pearl Harbor, HI

- S -

Ship	Hull	Home Port
Sacagawea	T-AKE 2	No home port
USS Safeguard	ARS 50	Sasebo, Japan
USS Saipan	LHA 2	Norfolk, VA
USS Salvor	ARS 52	Pearl Harbor, HI
Sampson	DDG 102	No home port
USS Samuel B. Roberts	FFG 58	Mayport, FL
USNS Samuel L. Cobb	T-AOT 1123	No home port
USS San Antonio	LPD 17	Norfolk, VA
San Diego	LPD 22	No home port
USS San Francisco	SSN 711	Guam
USS San Jacinto	CG 56	Norfolk, VA
USNS San Jose	T-AFS 7	No home port
USS San Juan	SSN 751	Groton, CT
USS Santa Fe	SSN 763	Pearl Harbor, HI
USNS Saturn	T-AFS 10	No home port
USS Scout	MCM 8	Ingleside, TX
USS Scranton	SSN 756	Norfolk, VA
USS Seawolf	SSN 21	Groton, CT

Ship	Hull	Home Port
USNS Seay	T-AKR 302	No home port
USS Sentry	MCM 3	Ingleside, TX
MV Sgt. Matej Kocak	T-AK 3005	No home port
MV Sgt. William R. Button	T-AK 3012	No home port
USS Shiloh	CG 67	Yokosuka, Japan
USS Shoup	DDG 86	Everett, WA
USS Shrike	MHC 62	Ingleside, TX
USNS Shughart	T-AKR 295	No home port
USS Simpson	FFG 56	Norfolk, VA
USNS Sioux	T-ATF 171	No home port
USS Sirocco	PC 6	Little Creek, VA
USNS Sisler	T-AKR 311	No home port
USNS Soderman	T-AKR 317	No home port
Somerset	LPD 25	No home port
USNS Spica	T-AFS 9	No home port
USS Springfield	SSN 761	Groton, CT
USS Squall	PC 7	Little Creek, VA
USNS Stalwart	T-AGOS 1	No home port
USS Stephen W. Groves	FFG 29	Pascagoula, MS
Sterett	DDG 104	No home port
USS Stethem	DDG 63	Yokosuka, Japan
USS Stout	DDG 55	Norfolk, VA
USNS Sumner	T-AGS 61	No home port
USNS Supply	T-AOE 6	No home port

- T -

Ship	Hull	Home Port
USS Tarawa	LHA 1	San Diego, CA
USS Taylor	FFG 50	Mayport, FL
USS Tennessee	SSBN 734	Kings Bay, GA
USS Texas	SSN 775	Groton, Conn.
USS Thach	FFG 43	San Diego, CA
USS The Sullivans	DDG 68	Mayport, FL
USS Theodore Roosevelt	CVN 71	Norfolk, VA
USS Thunderbolt	PC 12	Little Creek, VA
USNS Tippecanoe	T-AO 199	No home port
USS Toledo	SSN 769	Groton, CT
USS Topeka	SSN 754	San Diego, CA
USS Tortuga	LSD 46	Sasebo, Japan
Truxtun	DDG 103	No home port
MV TSgt. John A. Chapman	T-AK 323	No home port
USS Tucson	SSN 770	Pearl Harbor, HI
USS Typhoon	PC 5	Little Creek, VA

- U -

Ship	Hull	Home Port
USS Underwood	FFG 36	Mayport, FL

- V -

Ship	Hull	Home Port
USS Vandegrift	FFG 48	Yokosuka, Japan
USNS Vanguard	T-AG 194	No home port
USS Vella Gulf	CG 72	Norfolk, VA
USS Vicksburg	CG 69	Mayport, FL
USNS Victorious	T-AGOS 19	No home port
USS Virginia	SSN 774	Groton, CT

- W -

Ship	Hull	Home Port
USNS Walter S. Diehl	T-AO 193	No home port
USS Warrior	MCM 10	Ingleside, TX
USS Wasp	LHD 1	Norfolk, VA
USNS Waters	T-AGS 45	No home port
USNS Watkins	T-AKR 315	No home port
USNS Watson	T-AKR 310	No home port
Wayne E. Meyer	DDG 108	No home port
USS West Virginia	SSBN 736	Kings Bay, GA
USS Whidbey Island	LSD 41	Little Creek, VA
USS Whirlwind	PC 11	Manama, Bahrain
USS Winston S. Churchill	DDG 81	Norfolk, VA
SS Wright	T-AVB 3	No home port
USS Wyoming	SSBN 742	Kings Bay, GA

- Y -

Ship	Hull	Home Port
USNS Yano	T-AKR 297	No home port
USNS Yukon	T-AO 202	No home port

- Z -

Ship	Hull	Home Port
USNS Zeus	T-ARC 7	No homeport

20 December 2006, Pearl Harbor, Hawaii – Holiday lights shine from Arleigh-Burke class guided-missile destroyer USS Russell (DDG 59). Ships in Pearl Harbor will participate in the 2006 Holiday Light Competition. Regional commanders will judge the ships based on innovation, brilliance, enthusiasm, energy conservation, and overall categories. (U.S. Navy photo by Mass Communication Specialist James E. Foehl)